Contents

Foreword

It is a privilege for me to be chosen by my good friend Philip Castanza to write a foreword for *The Films of Jeanette MacDonald and Nelson Eddy.* It was my good fortune to be working at Metro-Goldwyn-Mayer during the time both were making their legendary films.

May I also add that it is an honor for me to be the honorary president of the Nelson Eddy Appreciation Society. I must admit I did know Nelson better, personally, than Jeanette, because we made a film together, *Rosalie,* which was a huge success at the box office. I will always be grateful to Jeanette for lending me her leading man.

Jeanette often visited me on the sound stages during my films, especially during dance sequences, and she had the most wonderful sense of humor. She was a perfect lady, gracious, feminine and very friendly—I adored her! For three years, starting in 1955, I did a television show for NBC called "Faith of Our Children," a religious Sunday School program (for which I received five Emmy Awards) and Jeanette was a guest on my show one Sunday (prior to her films she also was a Sunday school teacher). She brought her cameraman and makeup man to the studio—and how wise she was to do this, as she wanted to look her best at all times so as not to disappoint her public. She was a perfectionist in every sense of the word, both in her work and personally.

I cannot adequately express the ultimate joy and happiness that pervaded the set while filming *Rosalie* with Nelson. Here was a warm, sensitive, humorous, happy individual, just the opposite of the stoic, cardboard Canadian Mounted Policeman that many critics had labeled him. He played practical jokes on the set which had the crew and myself hysterical most of the time. Every day he brought one red rose to my dressing room (please don't misinterpret this—it wasn't for love—just his way of showing his appreciation for my talent). Mr. Louis B. Mayer abhorred blond men, and Nelson had a difficult time at

first in winning his approval. His vocal ability was outstanding, as Mr. Mayer knew, but L. B. wanted him to dye his hair (which Nelson was adamant about and would not comply with). In the end he became one of L. B.'s favorites in his stable of stars.

What can I say about the eight films that Jeanette and Nelson made that hasn't been said before?

When they sang they lifted your soul from an abyss to the highest floating cloud in the sky. To me they were what Lynn Fontanne and Alfred Lunt were to the spoken word and the drama of the theatre, they were what Pavlova and Nijinsky were to the dance world, they were the epitome of perfect blending and perfection. Both are gone now but they will never be forgotten—their music will live forever. Their recordings and cassettes will be a constant reminder of the magic and superb artists they were. How fortunate we are to have these legacies.

Jeanette is now reposing at Forest Lawn and Nelson at Hollywood Memorial Cemetery. Not far from Nelson is my dear Mother (who passed away recently) and each week I bring roses for her, and I always place a rose at Nelson's headstone, and another for Jeanette beside his, in memory and love.

ELEANOR POWELL

America's Singing Sweethearts

NAUGHTY MARIETTA

On March 29, 1935, MGM released its filmed version of Victor Herbert's immortal operetta, *Naughty Marietta*. It starred, for the first time, Jeanette MacDonald and a new leading man, Nelson Eddy. Overnight, the film was a runaway success! Thousands of letters poured into MGM's New York and Culver City offices, demanding to know more about the team and if they were to make another film together.

It was the era of the film closeup. A director crowded two faces, meticulously made up and carefully coiffured, into a small, square area draped with a rococo frame of richly lighted leaves and photographed them in deep, lush, soft-focus images. And, as the thoughtfully orchestrated musical score swelled, audiences in movie houses escaped the dreary world of poverty and unemployment just beyond the threshold of the lobby doors. What they watched on the screen seemed more real, more acceptable and more important than any other event in their mundane lives. Jeanette MacDonald and Nelson Eddy became a magical twosome who gave reality to fantasy. Those of us who were around when they reigned as the queen and king of Song can, at the mere mention of their names, become lost in yesterday.

Was it this magical transposition into a land of beauty, love and musical fantasy, during a time of bread lines, strikes, and general depression that made the team an overnight success? Was it the perfect blending of two voices never again to be equalled on the screen or stage that made the plots and characters seem more alive to the audience? Musical films were passé. But Warner Brothers' *Forty-Second Street*, 1933, had started a trend back to musical films, good musical films, not just an excuse to add sound to an old silent plot. Was *Naughty Marietta* just the frosting on the musical confection now in vogue or was the time just ripe for the American movie-going audience to take to their hearts a new set of sweethearts? Whatever it was, it was most effective for the stars, MGM and motion picture history.

Naughty Marietta was a project that had long been close to Louis B. Mayer's heart and he had waited patiently for just the right stars and the right director to come along before committing his dream to film. He first approached Jeanette MacDonald to do the film when she signed with MGM studios in 1934. She was only lukewarm to the idea and kept putting it off, due to the fact that there was no suitable leading man to play opposite her. After *The Merry Widow*, 1934, in which Jeanette proved herself so delightful in an operetta format, Mayer again approached her with the idea of doing *Naughty Marietta*. On the advice of his well-trusted girl Friday, Ida Koverman, Mayer asked Jeanette if she would agree to play opposite Nelson Eddy, a newcomer to Hollywood, but a seasoned artist in the concert world. Jeanette graciously gave Nelson co-starring status in their first film together, and America's Singing Sweethearts were born.

The only problem Mayer could foresee was how to present the operetta's most famous song, "Ah, Sweet Mystery of Life." By 1935, the song had become the theme song of Forest Lawn Cemetery and, as such, had become quite parodied in Hollywood. Under the careful guidance of Musical Director Herbert Stothart, the song was given a few "mentions" within the film but was saved for a climactic ending. It was Jeanette and Nelson's first duet* on the screen!

For director, Mayer assigned W. S. Van Dyke, then enjoying his first critical acclaim after having directed William Powell and Myrna Loy in a successful version of Dashiell Hammett's detective yarn, *The Thin Man*. Once again W. S. Van Dyke managed to create the kind of film magic to which audiences respond as two perfectly matched co-stars ignite sparks of rapport as one body of illuminated force. Such a phenomenon occurred between William Powell and Myrna Loy and Van Dyke managed to make cinematic lightning strike twice!

The nation, and the world, became operetta minded after the initial impact of *Naughty Marietta*. And if Powell and Loy seemed to be the personification of perfectly mated spouses, MacDonald and Eddy were the personification of all sweethearts.

Unlike Jeanette MacDonald, who had had five years of success and was well able to cope with her new-found superstardom, Nelson Eddy was always a little uncomfortable trying to live up to his cinema image. But, like Jeanette MacDonald, his "overnight success" was the culmination of many years of training and apprenticeship.

The success of *Naughty Marietta* had Louis B. Mayer in a state of mixed emotion attempting to find an acceptable script as a worthy follow-up for his musical mates. Nelson Eddy was scheduled to appear in a Technicolor version of *Rose Marie*, co-starring with Grace Moore. Miss Moore, still owing MGM a film, backed out of this project. Jeanette MacDonald was at liberty, awaiting the availability of Clark Gable to start filming *San Francisco*. Mayer immediately cast them in the re-make of Rudolf Friml's *Rose Marie*. Originally filmed as a 1928 silent starring Joan Crawford, the 1936 version was completely changed to suit Miss MacDonald's screen personality. The romantic male lead was shifted to the Royal Canadian Mountie, and as Sgt. Bruce, Nelson Eddy was cast in his most famous role. Jeanette was most beguiling as the opera star searching for her fugitive brother. And, Nelson, as the strong-jawed mountie determined to get his man, was the perfect foil. Adding to

MAYTIME

---

*Of the 37 various duets and reprises Jeanette and Nelson sang in their films—I think, this one most typified them. Others might have been photographed more beautifully, mounted more elaborately or vocally superior—but, to me, when I think of Nelson and Jeanette . . . I always visualize them on a staircase, singing this haunting duet.

ROSE MARIE

the film's appeal was some magnificent scenery, filmed on location at Lake Tahoe, which simulated the great Canadian Rockies. But it is their duet of the "Indian Love Call" which remains the most notable memory of *Rose Marie.* It's not too surprising that this scene is the one most remembered by the general public. Also, it is the most parodied of all MacDonald-Eddy numbers by comics and night club entertainers. Therefore, it was a poor choice as the only representative footage of their films in MGM's musical compilation, *That's Entertainment.*

On November 17, 1936, Jeanette MacDonald and Nelson Eddy stepped into the RCA Victor recording studios and made their first commercial recording. It was "Indian Love Call" backed with "Ah, Sweet Mystery of Life." It became an instant best seller and remained on RCA Victor's "101 Best Sellers" list for years. However, it took some twenty-five years before the artists received a gold record for the disc selling over a million copies! Upon receiving his gold record for "Indian Love Call," Nelson Eddy remarked, "That sure was a mighty slow Indian!"

Four days later, on November 21, 1936, they recorded three more duets, which were their only commercial recordings together for the next twenty-one years. They recorded "Will You Remember" backed with "A Farewell to Dreams" from their forthcoming film, *Maytime.* They also recorded "Song of Love" from Sigmund Romberg's operetta, *Blossom Time.* However, it was not released, until 1966 when RCA Victor released it in an LP album of "Jeanette MacDonald and Nelson Eddy" in its Vintage Series. Contrary to popular belief, these are the only commercial recordings Jeanette and Nelson made together during the height of their careers.

In 1938, after completing *Girl of the Golden West,* Nelson Eddy signed a new recording contract with Columbia Records. For the next twenty years he recorded exclusively with them, while Jeanette remained under exclusive contract with RCA Victor Records until her death. Thus it was virtually impossible for them to record any more duets or soundtrack albums of their co-starring films. In 1957, Nelson returned to RCA Victor Records and he and Jeanette recorded their first album together. It contained new recordings of "Ah, Sweet Mystery of Life," "Indian Love Call," and "Will You Remember." To the list of duets, they added their first commercial recording of "Wanting You." Entitled "Jeanette Mac-Donald and Nelson Eddy Favorites in Hi-Fi (Stereo)," neither of the stars' voices were up to the quality of their film soundtracks, nor were the arrangements or orchestra as plush as their MGM days. Even Miss MacDonald's choice of "The Breeze and I" seemed odd for her to sing or include in an album of favorites from their films. Never the less, the album was very successful and went into several pressings. Both stars were awarded a Gold Record, posthumously, for having sold over a million copies of the album.

By 1937, the team had become so popular that Irving Thalberg decided he was going to personally produce the stars' next film, *Maytime*. Sets were built, costumes designed and made and shooting started with Paul Lukas and Frank Morgan in key character roles. So great was the drawing power of the team at this time, Thalberg was filming the entire production in Technicolor. Then, suddenly Thalberg died and the production was scrapped.

An entire new production of *Maytime* was filmed, and in all ways it was far superior to the earlier production planned. Chief among its assets was a tightly written script, some exciting musical interludes, all expertly staged, and a very knowledgeable director, Robert Z. Leonard. Of Mr. Leonard, Miss MacDonald said, "He was not only one of the ablest directors but one who, being a singer himself, was deft and sympathetic in his handling of the musical phases of the story. He didn't believe in the iron-handed technique. Mr. Leonard always kept us pliable and spontaneous."

Subsequently, Jeanette MacDonald came to regard *Maytime* as her favorite film. Miss MacDonald has gone on record saying, "The role I like best of all those I have played was that of Marcia Mornay in *Maytime*. It had dramatic range such as is seldom offered an actress. The story took Marcia Mornay from the time she was an ingenuous, romantic girl of eighteen until she was a magnificent old grande dame of eighty. Besides the sweep of years encompassed in the part, Marcia's character underwent a development and a maturing process which was an actress' holiday. It was the kind of part which gives an actress use of all her powers in the characterization."

"At the time I was given the script of *Maytime*, I was known in the theatre and on the MGM lot as a singer—and as such, I was seldom given a role which required much more than singing. So as I became acquainted with Marcia Mornay, I liked her better than ever. More than a part, she represented my justification in striving to be a dramatic actress."

"Because *Maytime* was made the spring before Gene Raymond and I were married, it has been said that Marcia Mornay, which critics named my best performance, was sparked by the fact that I was deeply in love for the first time. Whatever the impetus, I consider Marcia Mornay my finest performance and my favorite role."*

NEW MOON

*In addition to being her favorite film role, *Maytime* provided Jeanette with another favorite, costumes. In a questionnaire, submitted by her fan club, Jeanette was asked which of all the costumes designed for her in her films was her favorite? She answered, "Many were very lovely, but I liked the ones from *Maytime* and *The Firefly* the best. The pink ballgown from the Louis Napoleon sequence in *Maytime*, being my singular favorite." Jeanette was at her loveliest in this costume, one of her most voluminous hoop-skirts. In watching the film, it is sheer joy just to watch Jeanette glide across the ballroom floor or up and down the grand staircase of the fantastic Court of Louis Napoleon set built by MGM. I can't think of any film actress, before or since, who wore costumes better or moved in them more graciously than Jeanette MacDonald. Be it the crinolines of *Naughty Marietta,* the hoops of *Maytime* or the Empire gowns of *The Firefly,* Jeanette seemed to be born in them with every fold of material moving as delicately as she did. Truly, she was the Princess Royal of all costume motion pictures.

MAYTIME

Happily for all MacDonald-Eddy fans, and MGM, 1938 saw two more-than-suitable properties filmed, uniting the stars. First, there was a lush new version of *The Girl of the Golden West*, filmed entirely in sepia-tone. David Belasco's play was used for the story line, but none of Puccini's music was used. Sigmund Romberg and Gus Kahn wrote an entire new score. Strangely, despite the film's length of 124 minutes, longer than most films at the time, and a score written especially for them, the stars were given no duets to sing! They only had a duet of a few bars at the end of the "Mariachie" production number and a short reprise of "Senorita." Fans felt a bit disappointed upon leaving the theatre. Where were the duets of *Marietta, Rose Marie,* and *Maytime*?

Sweethearts, the 1938 release made up in the music department, had some eleven duets and reprises for Jeanette and Nelson to sing, it is the most musical of all the MacDonald-Eddy films! It also had the added lure of Technicolor. It was MGM's first musical filmed entirely in the new three-color process of Technicolor. Critics and fans alike were united in thinking that all subsequent MacDonald-Eddy films should be filmed in color. Seen today, although the film is modern dress, only a twelve-gown fashion show dates the film. It still is witty and sparkling, and the musical numbers, mostly seen as productions on a stage, are as delightful as ever.

For over a year, the team of MacDonald-Eddy was not seen on the screen. In 1940, however, the singing sweethearts were back in each other's arms in re-makes of Sigmund Romberg's *New Moon* and Noel Coward's *Bitter Sweet. New Moon* had once served as a vehicle for Grace Moore and Lawrence Tibbett at a time when Louis B. Mayer had hopes of making them America's musical sweethearts. *Bitter Sweet* was lushly filmed in Technicolor but, much to the consternation of critics and fans, *New Moon* was not, although, ironically enough, the Moore-Tibbett version had been in color! *New Moon* is the superior film of their 1940 efforts, but neither that nor *Bitter Sweet* managed to generate the old excitement of a new MacDonald-Eddy feature. They had one more film left to make together. It was 1942's *I Married an Angel*, the film Jeanette MacDonald was to make as her first film under her new MGM contract in 1934. Somewhat smugly, Louis B. Mayer gave a rather stock reason for the decline of Jeanette MacDonald and Nelson Eddy: audiences had lost interest in the operatic film cycle because the advent of World War II was too real and too grisly for them to remain captivated by musical fantasies. Closer to the truth, however, are the actual facts that speak all to revealingly for themselves:

Having under contract two of the top commercial attractions in films, MGM felt their drawing power alone could carry the studio. Consequently instead of buying new properties for those stars, MGM starred them in four films which all had been made before. The late Fred Allen accurately termed this brand of production as "the termite philosophy of film making."

When Louis B. Mayer and his associates finally realized the error of their ways it was too late. For the last MacDonald-Eddy film together, MGM bought a top Broadway musical comedy, Rodgers and Hart's *I Married an Angel*. On Broadway, *I Married an Angel* delighted audiences with its youthful vivacity and sprightly choreography. On screen nothing could have been less suited to the ripe vocal talents of MacDonald and Eddy. Seen today, the film is a cute comedy. Being removed from the valentine world of their other films, we can more readily accept Jeanette and Nelson in this sophisticated romp. But on the total list of their films, it is the least popular and least rewarding.

Although Nelson and Jeanette remained active long after their halcyon days at MGM, they never made another film together after *I Married an Angel*. There was, however, always a rumor circulating around Hollywood that they would be reunited in a film. This almost came to pass when RKO managed to interest them in a film version of Sigmund Romberg's *East Wind* for which much pre-production planning was done. Eventually Howard Hughes, who had taken over the studio, rejected the project. Contract disputes, financial and script difficulties eventually defeated their plans to co-star in *Emissary from Brazil* which, at first, showed some promise of being a likely vehicle for them. Both Jeanette and Nelson regretted that this project did not come to fruition.

Although Jeanette MacDonald and Nelson Eddy never made another film together, through the years, they still appeared together professionally. During the years of World War II, they joined in several radio broadcasts. Chief of these were the "Lux Radio Theatre" presentations of *Naughty Marietta* on June 12, 1942 and *Maytime* on September 4, 1944. Jeanette made several appearances on Nelson's own weekly program, "The Electric Hour." She guest-starred on April 22, 1945 and again on December 16. Each time they did a different medley of the songs they had sung in some of their films. On April 7, 1946 and December 23, 1946, Jeanette again appeared as Nelson's guest on "The Electric Hour." For one of those performances, she was a last minute substitute for Gladys Swarthout who had taken suddenly ill.

"Lady Esther Screen Guild Theatre" was a popular half-hour radio program that adapted film successes into a half-hour format. On March 25, 1946 Jeanette and Nelson appeared in their first version of *Sweethearts* on this program. On December 15, 1947, they repeated this version of *Sweethearts* on "Lady Esther Screen Guild Theatre," only this time they sang the duet "Cricket On The Hearth," which was cut from the final print of the film. Their other appearance on this series was a June 23, 1946 broadcast of *Rose Marie*. The programs, a kind of mini version of "Lux Radio Theatre," never achieved the same succcess or popularity.

On December 20, 1956, Jeanette and Nelson made thier first TV

SWEETHEARTS

appearance together on the "Lux TV Show" over the NBC Network. Along with host Gordon MacRae, Jeanette and Nelson "guested" with Shirley Jones, Jack Cassidy, and Phil Harris. The theme of the program was "music from films." Jeanette soloed on "Beyond the Blue Horizon" while Nelson did a medley of "I Married an Angel," "At the Balalaika" and "Rosalie." During an ensemble with the other stars, Jeanette sang "I'll See You Again," Nelson "Rose Marie" and then they did a duet of "Will You Remember." The entire production ended with the entire cast singing "White Christmas."

Jeanette MacDonald and Nelson Eddy's last professional appearance together was on the TV show, "The Big Record," hosted weekly by Patti Page. Telecast on September 28, 1957 over the CBS Network, Jeanette soloed on "Italian Street Song," while Nelson sang "Out of the Night" and then they sang a duet of "Ah, Sweet Mystery of Life." It was a most fitting end to their years together to end with the duet they had sung some twenty-two years ago as the start of their association.

Through the years, when Nelson's night club act took him to Los Angeles or New York City and Jeanette was in town at the time, she and Gene always made sure to see at least one performance. As late as 1956, during Nelson's opening night at the Los Angeles Statler, Jeanette was at ringside. Between shows, she went backstage to greet Nelson and Gale Sherwood.

The MacDonald-Eddy union was certainly historic, but Nelson had reservations about himself. "Maybe if I had been younger," he said, "I could believe the nice things they said about me. But, I was thirty-four years old. I knew I was good, but I also knew I wasn't great."

Jeanette MacDonald and Nelson Eddy made a contribution so unique to the musical screen, they remain quite irreplaceable. As long as their films are shown on television and in theatrical reissue, it's comforting to know that "going to the movies" doesn't have to be a traumatic experience. And, it's rewarding to know that our youth, can also be mesmerized by the magic of old films, including the operettas of Jeanette MacDonald and Nelson Eddy.

On March 7, 1967, two years and fifty-one days after Jeanette's death on January 14, 1965, Nelson Eddy passed away. The last note of the great team was sung! The world will always be indebted to them for their delightful charm, their vocal beauty, and the hours of movie magic they created for us all. However, they will always be with us. For as long as films are shown and records are played, someone, somewhere will again be enchanted by America's Singing Sweethearts.

Forecourt, Grauman's Chinese Theatre, Hollywood

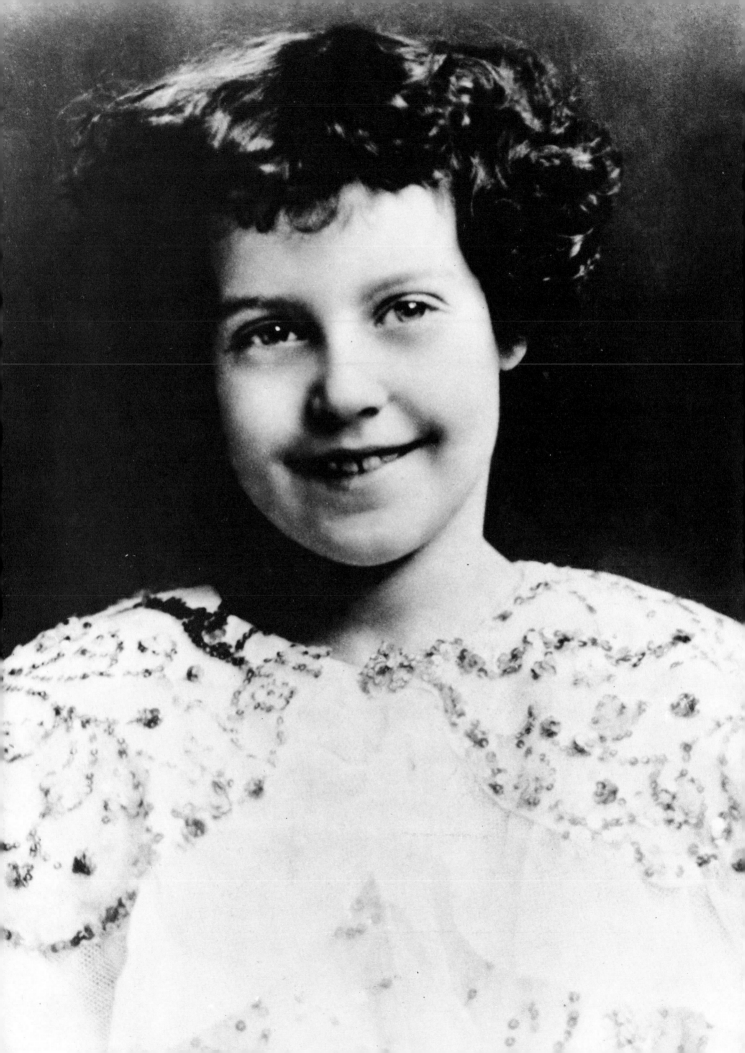

Jeanette MacDonald

Jeanette MacDonald, the youngest of the three daughters of Daniel and Anna, nee Wright, MacDonald, who lived in a red brick house in the old town of West Philadelphia, was born on Tuesday, June 18, 1907. Some sources insist the year was really 1903, while others say it was 1905. School records show both the 1903 and the 1907 dates. This could be the cause of some of the discrepancies, as could poor penmanship on these records. Even Jeanette's handwriting was not the most legible. Legend has it, Jeanette shaved the four years off her age when she wanted to get a start on Broadway. She was only fourteen–fifteen years of age by then, but she wanted to be an eleven-year-old chorus girl. By 1927, when she was at the height of her Broadway popularity she was only nineteen–twenty years old. She wanted to be a sixteen-year-old established star. Her birthdate on her marriage certificate to Gene Raymond and on her crypt in Forest Lawn's Hall of Freedom, her last resting place, states 1907—enough said.

Like her sisters Elsie and Blossom, Jeanette revealed a musical talent at a very early age so that close friends and neighbors referred to the girls as the "Lucky MacDonalds." Everyone remotely concerned with the MacDonald clan assumed each of the girls was destined for a theatrical success.

Their parents also thought their daughters exceptionally talented. So much so that Elsie and Blossom began dancing lessons at an early age and when Jeanette was five years old, she sang at a recital given by the dancing academy her sisters were attending. She was soon accompanying her sisters to dancing classes, and before too long she became the prima donna of the "Lucky MacDonald" sisters. But, by the time Jeanette was ten, the close-knit family had broken up.

Elsie, first to break the family circle, abandoned her promising musical career in an elopement-marriage. Soon Blossom left home to accept an offer to dance in a New York revue.

Jeanette remained with her parents in West Philadelphia and, in addition to continuous dancing lessons, she began singing lessons and the study of musical theory. By the time she was ten, she had memorized the "Jewel Song" from *Faust* by listening to a phonograph record. Family and friends alike were convinced that her dedication to pursuing a career in opera was absolute. Voice lessons, and dance instruction, continued on a daily basis and by the time she was twelve, she was teaching a Sunday School class. She later thought that the experience had given her the maturity to launch her theatrical career.

About a year later she accompanied her father, a contractor, on a business trip to New York City. Together, they went to see Blossom dance in Ned Wayburn's *Demi-Tasse Revue* at the Capitol Theatre. Jeanette's excitement and pride over her sister's accomplishment was so great, she all but ignored all her sister's questions

Jeanette at the age of three   Jeanette, five years old

about the family and friends in West Philadelphia. Jeanette watched Blossom's next performance from backstage. Her utter enchantment at being part of the theatrical scene, if only a back-stage observer, was immediately apparent to Ned Wayburn when he spotted her in the wings, and he wondered if this blue-green eyed, red haired beauty had any aspirations toward a stage career.

A brief conversation with her cleared up that point and Wayburn found himself wondering if such a young, seemingly awkward creature could pass a dance audition. He voiced these trepidations aloud and Jeanette begged only for a chance to show him what she could do. This was granted and Wayburn, no longer a cynical skeptic, hired her for a chorus spot.

This caused some excitement among the MacDonalds who finally concluded that they would have to pull up roots in West Philadelphia and move to New York City. Daniel MacDonald relocated his business interests and the family made the Gotham city their permanent home. Almost at once, however, MacDonald had cause to question his decision when the *Demi-Tasse Revue* closed soon after Jeanette joined its cast.

But, by the early 1920s, Jeanette had transferred from the Washington Irving High School in New York to the Julia Richman High School and was appearing in six shows a day at the Capitol Theatre in a new Wayburn revue. She soon advanced from the back row of the chorus line to the front, from an obscure understudy to understudy number one. She always arrived at the theatre wearing white cotton stockings and a middie blouse, usually out of breath. Before too long the other chorous girls had nicknamed her "Elsie Dinsmore."

Whether or not Ned Wayburn ever heard her referred to by that nickname, he cast her in a chorus spot of Jerome Kern's *The Night Boat* when producer Charles Dillingham hired him to stage that musical's elaborate dance numbers. Consequently, Jeanette, now a dazzlingly beautiful redhead, made her Broadway debut at the Liberty Theatre. Her stage presence was so overwhelming that later that year she was playing the second female lead in a touring company of *Irene*, where she got to sing the musical's hit song "Alice Blue Gown." And, by September of 1922, she had returned to Broadway to take over the lead in the long-running hit, *Tangerine* from departing star Martha Lober. A year later she opened, to critical acclaim, at the Greenwich Village Theatre in a revue called *A Fantastic Fricassee*. Praise for the show itself was less than enthusiastic, but the following year she was so successful in the role of Mitzi in *The Magic Ring* that she toured with it a year.

It was during this tour, in 1924, that her father died. One of his last wishes was for Blossom and Jeanette to continue their careers.

During 1923, Jeanette had become friendly with playwright Zelda Sears whose husband was the managing director of Henry

Savage's vast theatrical enterprises. Savage, an astute showman and a shrewd businessman, recognized Jeanette's ability and it was he who put her into *The Magic Ring*. Savage's contract with her was not exclusive and soon he was sharing her services with Sam and Lee Shubert. When the tour of *The Magic Ring* concluded, she was cast in the ingenue role of George and Ira Gershwin's *Tip Toes*. She vacillated between Savage and Shubert productions with four years of stardom in *Bubbling Over, Yes, Yes, Yvette,* and Hassard Short's musical comedy *Sunny Days*.

While appearing in the short-lived *Angela* during 1928, she was seen by screen actor Richard Dix who was so impressed with her beauty and stage presence that he implored Adolph Zukor, head of Paramount Pictures, to give her a screen test. Dix thought she would be the ideal leading lady for his next film, *Nothing But the Truth*. Jeanette made her screen test at Paramount's then New York Studio. Testing with her was another unknown screen possibility named Alexander Archibald Leach, later known as Cary Grant. Paramount decided Jeanette's screen test was below expectation and gave up the idea of her being Dix's leading lady, or anyone else's for that matter. (However, the screen test was not destroyed!) Mary Brian was finally cast in the part. Jeanette returned to work for the Shuberts in *Boom Boom*, taking the show on tour to Chicago.

Boom Boom fulfilled Jeanette's contract with the Shuberts so that when Ernst Lubitsch approached her (traveling all the way to Chicago to interview her) about casting her opposite Maurice Chevalier in *The Love Parade*, she was free to accept the offer. Some years later, at a Hollywood party, Lubitsch recalled being terrified of his first sound film assignment and the responsibility of finding the right leading lady, who could sing and dance, to co-star with Chevalier.

After testing several actresses, he was on the verge of signing Bebe Daniels when he happened to run Jeanette MacDonald's year-old test. The first time this test was screened for him, the wrong sound disc was sent along and by the time the right sound disc had been located the test film had been misplaced! Nevertheless, when disc and film were finally synchronized, Lubitsch knew he had his leading lady.

Paramount was equally enchanted with Lubitsch's selection and when she completed her costume tests for *The Love Parade* they signed Jeanette to a two-year contract. *The Love Parade* was a highly popular film. Chevalier's first film, *Innocents of Paris* was a mild success, but *The Love Parade's* profits and popularity exceeded it. It opened at the Criterion Theatre in New York City on November 19, 1929, with the elite of New York gladly paying eleven dollars a seat for the world premiere!

Jeanette became a popular movie star over night and the public

Jeanette (center) in Kiddie Revue Dutch number

Jeanette in 1927

In the 1927 stage play, *Yes, Yes Yvette*

was eager to see and hear more of her. So popular were her songs, "Dream Lover" and "March Of The Grenadiers" from *The Love Parade,* that RCA Victor Records signed her to an exclusive contract. On December 1, 1929, Jeanette entered the RCA Victor recording studios and cut her first commercial record.

Paramount then capitalized on her popularity by casting her opposite Dennis King in a lavish version of *The Vagabond King.* King, star of the original operetta on Broadway, was given his first starring role, and to insure success of the film, Paramount filmed the production in two-color process Technicolor.

In *Monte Carlo,* her co-star was Jack Buchanan and she popularized "Beyond The Blue Horizon" in one of the most imaginatively filmed sequences of the early sound era. Less memorable was Leo McCarey's *Let's Go Native* with Kay Francis and Jack Oakie.

Jeanette then free-lanced four films. *The Lottery Bride* for United Artists with a score by Rudolf Friml* and produced in two-color process Technicolor. For Fox studios she made *Oh, For a Man, Don't Bet on Women,* and, *Annabelle's Affairs.* Of all the films she made, Jeanette most disliked these three made for the Fox studios. Later she remarked, "At the time, movie musicals were out of vogue; and Winfield Sheehan, then head of the Fox studios, said 'No musicals!' I was limited to one song in each film and in one I didn't sing at all."

*Of all the popular operetta composers, Rudolf Friml was the one whose music Jeanette sang the most in her films. He composed the scores of Jeanette's films: *The Vagabond King, The Lottery Bride, Rose Marie,* and *The Firefly.* Sometime after Jeanette's funeral, Friml was asked why he didn't send a floral tribute to Jeanette. He replied that he did—"I gave her 'Only a Rose.'"

In the Broadway stage play *Boom Boom* with Frank McIntire, 1928

In 1931, she returned to Paramount, again to co-star with Maurice Chevalier in *One Hour with You*. Ernst Lubitsch wrote the script of *One Hour with You*, based on his silent hit *The Marriage Circle*, with MacDonald and Chevalier in mind and he assigned its direction to the very young George Cukor. But, things didn't go well, and he fired Cukor and completed the film himself. Then happily Jeanette was united with Chevalier in an exquisite musical comedy *Love Me Tonight*, brilliantly directed by Rouben Mamoulian. Script, supporting players, and songs were all first rate and *Love Me Tonight* remains the apex of Jeanette MacDonald's pre-Nelson Eddy career.

All of Miss MacDonald's Paramount features were well-mounted, visually handsome, and moderately successful. But, when the moment came for her to renew her contract, she declined and set sail for Europe.

By 1931, Jeanette had made some nine features (including *One Hour with You*, which was not released until 1932). She had become a very popular singing star both in America and Europe, where her films were also very popular. Never forgetting her goal of concert and opera, Jeanette undertook a series of concerts in London and Paris. These personal appearances, which commenced in 1931, were designed to squelch rumors, then circulating throughout Great Britain and Europe, that she had been killed in an automobile mishap! Thus her highly publicized appearances in London and Paris were occasions of double delight for her fans. Hollywood's first lady of song was, by now, well able to cope with the strenuous hours of the tour—and its success.

In 1933, Jeanette did a second concert tour of Europe, this time visiting France, the Netherlands, Belgium, and Switzerland. It was on this tour in Europe that Jeanette met Louis B. Mayer. Enchanted with her, he offered her an MGM contract. Metro, the most prestigious studio, offered her a larger salary, script approval and the services of their top costume designer, Adrian, as inducements. Any one of these things, or the combination, was too tempting for her to resist.

For her first film under his banner, Louis B. Mayer purchased a Broadway musical comedy, *I Married an Angel*, expressly for MacDonald. However, the newly-formed Hays Office thought the story line too "spicy" and the film was shelved. Instead, her first MGM musical was a lavish version of Jerome Kern's *The Cat and the Fiddle*, co-starring Ramon Novarro.

During her Paramount days, Miss MacDonald had an enviable camaraderie with director Ernst Lubitsch of whom she later said, "He could suggest more with a closed door than all the hayrolling you see openly on the screen nowadays." Miss MacDonald, however, did not share such a rapport with her co-star Maurice Chevalier.

While filming her second MGM film *The Merry Widow* (her

Greeted by Ernst Lubitsch upon her arrival in Hollywood.

Attending a preview in Hollywood with her manager Bob Richie

last co-starring role opposite Chevalier) Maurice's coolness generated into open hostility. Mayer had assigned Grace Moore as Chevalier's co-star for his lavish first sound version of *The Merry Widow*. Chevalier had expressed an early preference for Grace Moore as his co-star in several of his Paramount films. But, when it came to working in the same film, both argued over billing. Neither Moore nor Chevalier would take second billing to the other. It ended with Miss Moore walking out on the production. MGM, with all production preparations ready, cast Miss MacDonald in the title role, considering that MacDonald and Chevalier were a successful team at Paramount. This caused a chasm between the two musical talents, and the atmosphere during filming became uncongenial.

Chevalier's resentment of Miss MacDonald was not without foundation. Accustomed to being star absolute, he was well aware that she was receiving equal footage in their films and that she was being well received by the critics and the public. He also thought her something of a prude who was impervious to his Gallic charm. Frustrated by her rejection, his jealousy of her success was intense.

Oddly enough none of the strain shows in their film together. And while Miss MacDonald's greatest fame was to come after *The Merry Widow*, Chevalier's superstardom in Hollywood reached its zenith with that production. The following year, 1935, he made *Follies Bergere* at Fox and then returned to France.

The Merry Widow was so expensive that only a box-office miracle could have made it profitable. The film did not recoup enough to offset its production costs. It did, however, prove that Jeanette MacDonald was no longer the "lingerie queen" but the new "queen of the operettas."

San Francisco followed, and Jeanette will be remembered as one of the major contributors to the success of one of MGM's great films. It was also the first of her MGM films to have a song written especially for her. Over the years, the title song became associated with her as much as any of her operetta favorites.*

The year 1937 stands out as an exciting period in the life of Jeanette MacDonald. *Maytime,* her third film with Nelson Eddy was being heralded as their best. And, on June 16, she married screen actor Gene Raymond in a ceremony well covered and well recalled by both Louella Parsons and Hedda Hopper some twenty-

---

*On June 29, 1936, Jeanette made her first appearance on "Lux Radio Theatre." She starred in *Irene*. This time she did the lead, although she did once again sing "Alice Blue Gown." On January 25, 1937, she again appeared on "Lux Radio Theatre"— this time in the comedy/drama *Tonight or Never*, co-starring with Melvyn Douglas. During the 1937-1938 season on NBC Radio, Jeanette acted as Hostess on "Vicks Open House." Jeanette sang hits from her films, the operetta and concert worlds. She had a different guest on each week. . .a format Nelson used on his "Electric Hour" and "Kraft Music Hall" programs. Heavy Studio and concert commitments would not allow her to continue her radio career.

eight years after the event occurred.

It was one of Hollywood's most popular weddings, and certainly one of its most beautiful. The wedding ceremony, performed by the Reverend Wilsie Martin, at the Wilshire Methodist Episcopal Church, in Beverly Hills, was prefaced by Nelson Eddy singing "I Love You Truly." Jeanette's gown, designed for her by MGM's costume designer, Adrian, was pale pink, her favorite color. Her attendants, her sister Blossom (Rock), Fay Wray, Ginger Rogers, Helen Ferguson and Mrs. Johnny Mack Brown all wore pink also, and walked down an aisle arched with fresh pink roses. Gene's best man was his brother, Robert Marlow, and ushers Nelson Eddy, Allan Jones, Johnny Mack Brown, Basil Rathbone, Warren Rock (Blossom's husband), Harold Lloyd, and Richard Hardgreaves. More than 10,000 fans outside the church caused such a traffic jam that the bridesmaids were forty minutes late. Inside, 1,000 guests awaited amongst a bower of pink roses and countless lighted candles.

Before embarking on a Hawaiian honeymoon, the newlyweds were given a lavish reception by Basil and Ouida Rathbone, which, in fact, was a double celebration since this reception was also to honor another pair of famous newlyweds, Mary Pickford and Charles "Buddy" Rogers.

Allan Jones, a most embarrassed usher at Jeanette's wedding (his shoes squeaked) became her co-star in her next film, *The Firefly*. Nelson Eddy, meantime, made—two pictures with two new leading ladies—Eleanor Powell starred with him in Cole Porter's *Rosalie* and Ilona Massey joined him in *Balalaika*. Both films were substantial successes and Louis B. Mayer was delighted that each star had a strong enough box-office following to appear solo to offset the times when no suitable tandem script was available.

1939 saw Jeanette MacDonald crowned "Queen of Hollywood" by a nationwide poll in Ed Sullivan's newspaper columns. Ed Sullivan, himself, presented the crown to her and her reigning king, Tyrone Power. To cash in on her popularity, MGM starred her in another solo film *Broadway Serenade*. This time, the magic didn't work! The music was good, but the plot was thin and Lew Ayres was miscast. Busby Berkeley made his MGM debut with this film. However, his style did not mesh with the style of Jeanette MacDonald.

After the strong success of *New Moon* and the milder one of *Bitter Sweet,* Jeanette was given the choice of co-starring again with Nelson in a film version of *The Chocolate Soldier* or appearing on her own in a musical version of *Smilin' Through*. Miss MacDonald made a valiant effort to regain some of her box-office stature by electing to star in the new version of *Smilin' Through* which also had the added appeal of a strong co-starring role for her husband, Gene Raymond. Its general release date of December 7, 1941 didn't enhance its appeal to the public, who were now more inter-

Jeanette and Gene on their wedding day, June 16, 1937

Lily Pons, Jeanette, Rosa Ponselle, Grace Moore, John McCormack, and Gladys Swarthout attending a premiere of *That Girl From Paris*

With Hedda Hopper

ested in World War II than World War I.

Miss MacDonald's fortunes were no better in *Cairo,* a spy comedy she did with Robert Young and Ethel Waters. When the time came to sign a new contract with MGM, she decided to retire temporarily from films. She kept professionally active, however, with radio work, recordings, and concert tours.

In the spring of 1939, Jeanette started the first of her cross-country concert tours. Everywhere she went, she broke existing records! 1940 saw another concert tour that ended with her first concert in Los Angeles, now her home town. She soon became the biggest box-office draw in the concert world. 1942 saw her in two concert tours across the United States. She donated all the proceeds from her spring concert, $94,681.87, to the Army Emergency Relief Fund. That summer she toured seven states entertaining service men in Army camps. One critic wrote, "With her golden voice, shining spirit, moonglow personality and titian hair, Miss MacDonald brings light into any auditorium, even in the darkness of a world at war." Gene Raymond, meanwhile, was serving in the Army Corps as a lieutenant.

On May 8, 1943, under the coaching of the Metropolitan's Leon Rothier, Jeanette made her grand opera debut at His Majesty's Theatre in Montreal, Canada by singing the role of Juliet in Gounod's *Romeo and Juliet.* Armand Tokatyan sang Romeo and Ezio Pinza was Friar Laurence. Then, coached by Lotte Lehmann, she repeated her Juliet role at the Chicago Civic Opera House on Saturday, November 4, 1944, thus making her U.S. opera debut.

Like Nelson Eddy, she devoted much of her time between such appearances, to touring military installations and entertaining servicemen. The G.I.'s enthusiasm for Miss MacDonald's songs was equalled only by the excitement of a glimpse of Betty Grable's million dollar legs. She continued her concerts throughout the United States with sell-outs everywhere she went. Audiences stood in line for blocks and for hours to see their favorite star. At her August, 1943, open-air concert she shattered attendance records in Milwaukee, Wisconsin, where she made her debut as a guest soloist with a symphony orchestra. 42,000 attended, topping the existent record by 12,000.

In 1944, Jeanette returned to the screen, but this time to Universal Studios. It was her first film away from MGM in ten years! Jeanette "guest starred" as herself with an all-star cast in *Follow the Boys.* Jeanette sang "Beyond the Blue Horizon," which she had first introduced fourteen years earlier, and "I'll See You in My Dreams." The war years over, Jeanette continued her tours of the Army Camps and concert tours, and in 1946 she went to the British Isles. Just before Jeanette MacDonald started filming *Three Daring Daughters,* in 1947, her mother died of a heart attack at the age of 70. The loss was a great shock. Anna MacDonald followed her

Jeanette and her mother in late 30's (after being named Queen of the Movies)

Jeanette with her mother and Gene with his brother and mother

27

(Left) With Tyrone Power
receiving their crowns as King
and Queen in a film popularity
poll

With Gene Raymond and Irene Dunne

Adrian checks out his costume he designed for Jeanette on the
New Moon set

With Fredric March, Gene Raymond, Anita Louise and Harold Lloyd

With Gene Raymond on stage in a scene from the stage production of *The Guardsman*, 1951

Making her opera debut in *Romeo and Juliet* with Ezio Pinza, Toronto, 1943

daughter's career very closely and lived with Jeanette until her death. Burial was in Philadelphia.

In 1947, Louis B. Mayer persuaded Jeanette to return to films and to MGM. He gave her a script entitled *The Birds and the Bees,* in which Jeanette played a mother with three growing daughters. Her male co-star was to be Jose Iturbi. Released in 1948, the title was changed to *Three Daring Daughters.* It was well received, being MGM's seventh top-grossing film of the year. The same cannot be said of Jeanette's second film of that year, *The Sun Comes Up.* Co-starred with Lloyd Nolan, it was also a vehicle for the dog Lassie. It was Jeanette's last film for MGM and the last motion picture she was to make. It has been said that many a great star's last film turns out to be a dog, but it was truly a shame for MGM to star their song queen with a dog in her last film.

Until her death, Jeanette MacDonald never forsook her career. In 1949, she did four radio "Railroad Hour" performances with Gordon MacRae. She did *Naughty Marietta,* January 17th; *Bitter Sweet,* January 31st; *The Merry Widow,* March 7th and *Apple Blossoms,* April 18th. On November 13, 1950, she made her television debut as a guest soloist on "The Voice of Firestone." 1951 saw her co-starring with Gene Raymond in a revival of *The Guardsman* in which they toured for fifteen weeks. Gene Raymond wrote special lyrics to "Clair de Lune" for Jeanette to sing during the performance of *The Guardsman.* She appeared on such TV shows as "The Toast of the Town," "The Ken Murray Show," and a citation program on "Toast of the Town" with Gene Raymond. And, she made her last opera appearance in *Faust* with the Philadelphia Grand Opera Company.

On November 12, 1952, Jeanette was surprised by Ralph Edwards on his television show, "This Is Your Life." Guests included Gene, Nelson Eddy, her sisters, Blossom and Elsie, Grace Newell, her singing coach, Miss Edna Clear, her seventh grade English teacher, and a sailor she danced with at the Hollywood Canteen during the war years.

Jeanette, always a staunch Republican was invited by President Eisenhower, to sing at a White House dinner in November, 1954. After the formal dinner, Jeanette was summoned to the ballroom, where the chairs were arranged like a small theatre. Her program consisted of the waltz from *Romeo and Juliet,* "Le Miroir," "The Kerry Dancers," "The Last Rose of Summer," "From a Very Little Sphynx," "Un Bel Di, Vedremo" from *Madame Butterfly* and "Will You Remember." As a special request from the president she sang "Italian Street Song" as an encore. At the second Inaugural Ball in January of 1957, Jeanette was again requested to sing by President Eisenhower. She sang "The Star Spangled Banner" and later "Will You Remember" and "Giannina Mia".

May 30, 1953, Jeanette was given an honorary degree, Doctor of Music, at Ithaca College in New York. In the spring of 1953

President Eisenhower and members of his family meet celebrities who took part in the festivities at the Inaugural Ball of January 21, 1953 in Washington, D.C. Left to right: Guy Lombardo, Fred Waring, Mrs. John S. Doud (the President's mother-in-law), Tony Martin, Jeanette, Mrs. Mamie Eisenhower, James Melton, President Dwight D. Eisenhower, Lily Pons and George Murphy

As Anna in a scene from the stage production of *The King and I*, 1956 in summer stock

Welcoming Eleanor Steber and Rise Stevens of the Metropolitan Opera to Hollywood on their concert tour and vacation

Jeanette made her night club debut at the Sands Hotel in Las Vegas, Nevada. She took her night club act to the Coconut Grove in Hollywood in the spring of 1954. That summer, Jeanette made her summer stock debut, appearing with Glenn Burris in *Bitter Sweet* at Evansville, Indiana; Louisville, Kentucky; Pittsburgh, Pennsylvania; and St. Charles, Illinois. She repeated this role at the Dallas, Texas State Musicals in 1955. At the American Composers' Festival, she and Glen Burris did a concert version of *Show Boat*.

Jeanette and Gene Raymond began 1956 by being the official hostess and host of the Tournament of Roses Parade. Television saw Jeanette twice on "Masquerade Party" once dressed as "Old MacDonald who had a farm;" and on February 1, 1956 she appeared on the "Screen Directors Playhouse" production of "Prima Donna," written especially for her by Gene Raymond. She sang the waltz from *Romeo and Juliet* and "I Had a Dream, Dear." On August 20, 1956, Jeanette opened in *The King and I* in Kansas City, Missouri. She wanted very badly to do the film version for 20th Century Fox in 1954, but Deborah Kerr was chosen for the role.

Jeanette and Gene Raymond appeared on television in a "Playhouse 90" version of *Charley's Aunt* with Art Carney in the lead on CBS March 28, 1957. And October 31, she and Gene were Edward R. Murrow's guest on "Person To Person." Her last professional appearance was with Gene in the Canadian TV production of "Flashback" on June 22, 1963.

Through the years she had been affected by a recurring heart murmur. The condition became acute and in 1963, at the Methodist Hospital in Houston, Texas, she underwent surgery for an arterial transplant. Her recovery was sufficient to announce her intention to star in a musical version of *Sunset Boulevard*. Jeanette would portray a fading opera star, instead of the original fading movie star, and she was to sing some songs from her past hits as well as new compositions. It was planned for a 1965 Broadway opening. But, after a series of minor heart attacks she returned to the Houston hospital, early in January of 1965, for open-heart surgery. Her condition worsened rapidly.

Gene Raymond never left her side during her illness. On January 14, she opened her eyes for a moment, looked at her husband, and smiled wanly. "I love you," she told him. "I love you too," he replied. And Jeanette MacDonald closed her eyes forever.

Part of the service, at Forest Lawn Cemetery, included the playing of Jeanette's recordings of "Ave Maria" and "Ah, Sweet Mystery of Life," selected by her husband, and piped through loudspeakers for the people across the street from the chapel who came to pay their respects. The list of honorary pallbearers included: former Presidents Eisenhower and Truman, Richard M. Nixon, Chief Justice Earl Warren, Associate Justice Tom Clark, Alfred

Hitchcock, Ronald Reagan, Spencer Tracy and Nelson Eddy. Members of the family and close friends attending the funeral included her two surviving sisters, Mrs. Blossom Rock, and Elsie Schreiter, Ralph Edwards, Mrs. Nelson Eddy, Gale Sherwood, Allan Jones, Greer Garson, Jane Powell, General Lauris Norstad, Irene Dunne, Mary Pickford, and Charles "Buddy" Rogers, Thomas Jackson, Z. Wayne Griffith, Jack Oakie, Joe E. Brown, Lew Ayres, Buddy Ebsen, Leon Ames, Otto Kruger, Meredith Willson, Lauritz Melchior, Reginald Denny, Jose Iturbi, Robert Armbruster, Robert Ballen, Senator George Murphy, Barry Goldwater, his daughter and son-in-law Richard Holt, Johnny Mack Brown, Joe Pasternak, Wilfred Pelletier and Virginia Grey.

Lloyd Nolan delivered the eulogy at the Church of the Recessional on January 18, 1965 at 2:00 P.M. Interment was in the Hall of Freedom in Forest Lawn Memorial Park, Glendale, California.

Some two years later, during an interview, Nelson Eddy had this to say about his illustrious co-star: "I play her records and she is as alive to me as she ever was."

Nelson Eddy

Nelson Eddy was born on June 29, 1901, in Providence, Rhode Island, and could trace his ancestry back to the first colonists. The family name had originally been spelled Eddye, but after two generations here, the final vowel was dropped. According to Nelson, his family did not come over on the *Mayflower*—they missed it by ten years.

Nelson's father was an electrical engineer and an inventor of naval devices. For fourteen years he served the U.S. Torpedo Station at Rhode Island. He was a veteran of the Spanish-American War.

Nelson's mother, Isabel Kendrick Eddy, was born and brought up in Atlanta, Georgia.

Nelson had a childhood rich with music. His parents were church soloists; his paternal grandfather was a bass drummer in the Reeves band for fifty years; his maternal grandmother was a famous oratorio singer. Nelson had his early schooling at the Dartmouth Street Primary School in New Bedford, Massachusetts. Entering the first grade at the age of five, he gradually participated musically in school plays, displaying a flair for playing the drums. The family moved to Providence where Nelson's parents both took an active part in amateur theatricals doing many Gilbert and Sullivan operettas. His mother was also soloist in Grace Church. It was natural that Nelson should be singing in the same church in the boy's choir, between the ages of 9 and 14.

In 1915 his parents separated and his mother took him to live in Philadelphia where Nelson took a job with Mrs. Eddy's brother who managed the Mott Iron Works. Nelson never returned to school after this move. He began as a switchboard operator and had a series of jobs until he left to work for two newspapers, the *Philadelphia Press* and the *Public Ledger and Evening Bulletin*. Some of his jobs were writing obituaries, covering "baseball games and murders," cashier and night clerk. In 1920, he started a year's employment as a copywriter for N. W. Ayer and Sons, a Philadelphia advertising agency.

Strangely enough, when Nelson Eddy moved to Philadelphia and was studying music there, going to concerts, appearing in amateur productions, he never met his future co-star, Jeanette MacDonald, who was living and studying music there at the same time. And neither he nor Jeanette ever met their other co-star at MGM, Allan Jones, who also hailed from Philadelphia.

Nelson's father and mother were married December 23, 1899, and divorced April 24, 1918. William Eddy remained in Providence and later married Marguerite Elliot in the chapel at Vassar College on June 13, 1923. Virginia, Nelson's half-sister, was born of that union on February 21, 1925. She became Mrs. J. Lloyd Brown of Pawtucket, Rhode Island and her two sons were favorite nephews to Nelson through the years.

Nelson was a self-educated man, both intellectually and musi-

Nelson Eddy at six months

At the age of 21   As a young choirboy

As Amonasro in Verdi's opera *Aida*

cally. He studied hard and took numerous correspondence courses. He began learning operatic roles by listening to the records of the great singers, in the home of a friend. Hence, it might be said that Ruffo, Amato, Scotti, Campanari, and such great baritones were his early vocal teachers.

His first appearance on the stage was on January, 1922, in Mrs. George Dall Dixon's society musical play *The Marriage Tax,* at the Academy of Music. Nelson played the King of Greece with smashing success. By accident, his name was omitted from the program. It was a stroke of luck because the next day all the critics wrote him up, wanting to know who the baritone was with the marvelous voice! This appearance with a semi-professional company sparked him into taking singing lessons, and a year later he was giving a concert in Philadelphia.

His first music teacher was David Bispham, a famous baritone for the Metropolitan Opera Company. Totally untrained, he sang for Mr. Bispham and asked for help. Bispham was overwhelmed at Nelson's voice and agreed to teach him. Through Bispham, Nelson became a member of the Savoy Company, a group dedicated to presenting the works of Gilbert and Sullivan. He first performed publicly with the Savoy Company at the Broad Street Theatre in Philadelphia as Strephon in *Iolanthe* in May, 1922. He remained with the Savoy group for the next two years, maintaining a grueling schedule of lessons, rehearsals, and performances.

Such determination paid off, and in 1924 he joined the Philadelphia Civic Opera Company. His first role with them was Amonasro in *Aida.* Alexander Smallens, musical director of the Philadelphia Civic Opera Company, became interested in Nelson and gave him serious coaching. Under Smallens' guidance, he sang some twenty-eight leading operatic roles. Midway, the Philadelphia Civic became the Philadelphia Grand Opera. In the latter company was a singer who became a friend and teacher to Nelson, Edouard Lippe. He was instrumental in appreciating Nelson's potential. It was he who suggested Nelson study with William Vilonat, the internationally celebrated teacher.

Vilonat had to return to his native Dresden. Nelson having advanced under his tutelage wished very much to go and study with him abroad. As Nelson was very poor and working with an advertising company, he went to a friend who was a banker in Philadelphia and obtained a loan, which he paid back in full, within six years time. Each year for three years thereafter, Nelson went abroad to study with Vilonat until his death.

Nelson made his New York debut as Tonio in *Pagliacci* at the Metropolitan Opera House in 1924. Then followed his tenure with the Philadelphia Opera Company working under the direction of such masters as Fritz Reiner and Leopold Stokowski. On November 24, 1931, Stokowski again conducted when he sang at the New York Metropolitan Opera House in *Wozzeck,* in the drum major role.

In costume for a 1927 stage appearance

In 1928, he signed with Arthur Judson of Columbia Concerts and made his first concert appearance in Norristown, Pennsylvania. Concert after concert followed and Nelson developed a reputation in the musical world. By 1932, Nelson had twenty-eight operas and eleven oratorios in his repertoire besides countless numbers of art songs, popular classics and, yes, even operetta favorites.

Nelson continued concertizing under the management of Judson, O'Neill, Judd and appeared in the Community Concert series, often with symphony orchestras. While on concert tour on the West Coast, in San Diego, he was sent a desperate emergency call to replace the great artist Lotte Lehmann (who later coached Jeanette MacDonald for her U.S. opera debut), who was taken ill before her concert in Los Angeles.

"It was a brilliant success," one Los Angeles newspaper reported, "with the baritone responding to no less than fourteen encores and innumerable curtain calls."

A talent scout for RKO was among those who attended the performance and he came backstage to offer Nelson a screen test. When Paramount heard the news, they also approached him for a screen test. It was, however, Nelson Eddy's third screen test, ten days after his appearance at the Philharmonic auditorium, that lead directly to his stardom in motion pictures. This third test came about through the machinations of Louis B. Mayer's executive assistant, Ida Koverman, who had also attended the concert. She reported not only her own enthusiasm to her boss, but also the fact that Paramount and RKO had tested him, and Mark Sandrich of RKO, had offered him a minimum players contract which Eddy had rejected.

The contract finally negotiated by Eddy and Mayer called for his exclusive services for seven years. Included in the contract, was the provision that Nelson could take three months of every year to continue his concertizing. No matter how demanding his film roles became, they never were allowed to interfere with his annual concerts. In this instance, Nelson differed from Jeanette MacDonald. Jeanette had worked in films for ten years, becoming a famous film star, before her studio would let her concertize between film productions.

Before he was discovered in films, Nelson was on radio for the "Hoffman Hour," followed by the G. E., Firestone, Chase and Sanborn programs and several others including the "Telephone Hour." He did his own "Electric Hour," Vicks and the Old Gold weeklies.

While Nelson had a satisfactory contract, he had to wait two years before he appeared on the screen. His first assignment was one musical number in Joan Crawford's *Dancing Lady*, a film also notable for the screen debut of Fred Astaire. Nelson appeared in the finale and sang "Rhythm of the Day." Since he was unaccustomed to working without an audience and post-synchronizing his song to match his lip movements, Nelson was not comfortable in this tech-

Ann and Nelson Eddy, 1939

With soprano Lotte Lehman on the set of *The Chocolate Soldier*

37

With Jeanette, Gene Raymond,
Edgar Bergen and Charlie McCarthy
on the Chase and Sanborn radio
show

nique and he may have seemed wooden to some people. For reasons known only to MGM, *Dancing Lady's* release date was held up after the film was completed. Consequently, Nelson's second feature, 1934's *Broadway to Hollywood,* is often listed as his first film, but it was 1933's *Dancing Lady,* starring Joan Crawford and Clark Gable.

Nelson Eddy's state of mind wasn't improved when he was cast in similar assignments in *Broadway to Hollywood* (with Frank Morgan and Alice Brady, in which he sang a concert number with Ted Paxton accompanying him on the piano) and *Student Tour,* 1934, starring Jimmy Durante. Nelson had a small part playing himself and singing "The Carlo." He was displeased with his screen image which he called "negative." But, when he asked to be released from his contract, Louis B. Mayer placated him by saying all he needed was additional dramatic training, the right script, the right director, and the right co-star!

"I engaged a dramatic coach," Eddy later recalled, "and began to study the techniques of acting on the screen. That same day I also discovered how little I really knew. . . ." After the enormous success of *Naughty Marietta,* he returned to what he did know, and he took his first leave for his concert work. He was a phenomenal success, drawing crowds everywhere. He sang before an audience of 10,000 in White Plains, New York, and on March 17, 1935 he gave a recital at New York's Town Hall.

At the 1939 opening of the Los Angeles Opera Season at the Shrine Auditorium, Madame Amelita Galli-Curci and Nelson are shown arriving for the event

With Shirley Temple at a special Christmas show

Nelson paints a portrait of his leading lady, Jeanette

Nelson cementing his footprints at Grauman's Chinese Theatre in Hollywood

SWEETHEARTS

MAYTIME

Rose Marie and *Maytime* followed, and in 1937, Nelson made his first starring film without Jeanette MacDonald, *Rosalie*. Originally an operetta by Sigmund Romberg, *Rosalie* was purchased by MGM Studios, where only its title and West Point setting were retained. The original plot and most of Romberg's music was dropped in the film transition. Louis B. Mayer commissioned Cole Porter to write an entirely new musical score, with specific instructions to write a song for Nelson Eddy as close to "Rose Marie" as possible! "Rosalie" was the result. It had a delightful cast including Frank Morgan, Edna May Oliver, and Ray Bolger, but it was the beautiful blonde newcomer from Budapest, Hungary, Ilona Massey, here making her American debut, who claimed the best notices. *Rosalie* proved a success. The film remains famous for Eleanor Powell's dance sequence on the drums, which enjoyed new popularity in MGM's musical extravaganza *That's Entertainment.*

The year 1938 saw Nelson reunited with Miss MacDonald in *The Girl of the Golden West* and *Sweethearts,* his first film in color. His two films without Miss MacDonald, released during 1939, were *Let Freedom Ring,* with Virginia Bruce and Victor Mc-Laglen, and *Balalaika,* with Ilona Massey in co-starring status this time. Both films were moderately successful.

The marriage of Nelson Eddy and Ann Denitz Franklin (January 9, 1939) started out to be a quiet affair, a secret elopement to Las Vegas because Nelson was afraid the studio would look askance on his marriage. Those were the days when handsome bachelor stars remained bachelors, to maintain the romantic image. Studios were very jealous of all their male stars. But when the news became known, the press was sensational. The elopement was front page news in three-inch letters in newspapers all over the country, especially in Los Angeles. This assuaged any feelings the studio had about their bachelor stars marrying. Many later-day male stars were indebted to Nelson's breakthrough with the studio on this point!

The marriages of both Nelson Eddy and Jeanette MacDonald have proven over the years to be very happy unions and each lasted until the end of their lives.

Off screen Nelson led a quiet life. His chief hobby was collecting pewter. He also enjoyed working in sculpture and painting in oils. Often, between takes on a film, he sat alone in his dressing room working on sketches, portraits, or busts of his co-stars. Most notable of these was a lovely oil portrait Nelson did of Jeanette on the set of *Bitter Sweet.* A bust he sculptured of Susanna Foster between takes on *The Phantom of the Opera* was used as an actual prop within the film.

Between film assignments, Nelson continued making notable concert tours and doing radio work. In June, 1939, the American Institute of Cinematography bestowed on Nelson Eddy the Award of Achievement and an honorary membership in recognition of his distinguished contribution in advancing the standards of musical interpretation in motion pictures. In 1939 and 1940, he was elected "Star of Stars" in Radio Guild's poll. On October 19, 1939, he was guest star with Leopold Stokowski in a Los Angeles concert for Polish War Relief. It was the first in a long line of war benefit performances.

The film-going public was happy to have Nelson Eddy and Jeanette MacDonald back together in *New Moon* and *Bitter Sweet*. It prompted MGM to plan still another vehicle for the stars. On the agenda was a film version of Oscar Straus' *The Chocolate Soldier*. However, George Bernard Shaw wanted too high a price to use his original play *Arms and the Man*. Louis B. Mayer would not compromise and the film ended up as a musical version of *The Guardsman*. The film retained the title *The Chocolate Soldier* (since Shaw didn't own the copyright on that) and all of Straus' music. *The Guardsman* served as a very successful play for Alfred Lunt and Lynn Fontanne on the stage and in a 1930 MGM film. Nelson was fortunate in having the opportunity to make a film based on this brilliant work. Critics and audiences alike found this film a true musical comedy. Co-starring with Nelson was Rise Stevens of the Metropolitan Opera in her screen debut. Unfortunately, Miss Stevens suffered comparisons with Jeanette MacDonald and even ended up in costumes originally designed for Miss MacDonald.

Accompanied by Ted Paxton, Nelson sang at the Inaugural Gala for Franklin D. Roosevelt, at Constitution Hall on January 19, 1941. On January 27, 1941, the University of Southern Calfornia bestowed on Nelson the Master of Music degree.

Nelson Eddy was more actively involved in radio work than Miss MacDonald. Beginning in 1937, he had been a regular on "The Chase And Sanborn Hour" show which, hosted by Don Ameche, starred Edgar Bergen and Charlie McCarthy. It was one of the airways, most popular programs. In the beginning, Nelson's contribution to each show was a song or two. Later, his services were expanded. Recalls Edgar Bergen, "He never seemed to be able to unbend enough to tell a joke. We made a joke out of the fact that every time Nelson tried a funny story, it fell flat." This condition was a temporary one and Nelson developed an expert flair for comedy. A few critics felt this radio training most helpful in delivering some wonderful comic moments to *The Chocolate Soldier*.

Unfortunately an opportunity to do screen comedy never occurred again. The critics and Nelson's fans did not think *I Married an Angel* anywhere near as clever or amusing as *The Chocolate Soldier*, although it had some delightful moments. *I Married an Angel* completed Nelson's contract with MGM and he left the studio in July of 1942. Nelson and Jeanette never got to film some of the properties MGM especially bought for them. In 1936, MGM

NEW MOON

SWEETHEARTS

MAKE MINE MUSIC

With Father Peyton, Gregory Peck and friend on the Armed Forces Command Performance shows

announced Jeanette and Nelson would co-star in a dramatic version of *The Prisoner of Zenda.* MGM then sold it to David O. Selznick, who filmed it in 1937 with Ronald Colman and the lovely Madeleine Carroll. Selznick then sold it back to MGM, who refilmed it in 1952 with Stewart Granger and Deborah Kerr. In the meantime, there was talk of filming the musical version, *Princess Flavia* with Miss MacDonald. In 1940, MGM bought the screen rights to *Show Boat* from Universal for a re-make with Jeanette and Nelson. The project never came to pass, and in 1951, MGM made a color version starring Kathryn Grayson and Howard Keel, the 1950s version of MacDonald and Eddy.

From Paramount, MGM purchased the rights to *The Vagabond King* for Nelson and Jeanette. "Song of the Vagabonds," from *The Vagabond King's* score, was one of Nelson's favorite selections on many of his radio programs. This project, too, never came to pass. And, finally MGM sold *The Vagabond King* back to Paramount, where it was remade in 1956 with Kathryn Grayson and Oreste.

In 1943 Nelson co-starred with Susanna Foster and Claude Rains in a remake of Lon Chaney's horror film, *The Phantom of the Opera.* Nelson defined his characterization, originally played by Norman Kerry in 1925, with a nice light touch and an ample sampling of brilliantly staged musical numbers. Borrowing an idea successfully used in *Maytime,* Universal's music department, "composed" two special operas for use within the plot line of the story. As in *Maytime,* one opera used the music of Tchaikovsky, based on themes from his "Fourth Symphony," and the other, the French opera, used themes of Chopin.

The making of *The Phantom of the Opera* has an ironic note to it. The other male singer in Hollywood, at the time, who would have been an ideal choice for the romantic lead in the film was Allan Jones. Jones was then under contract to Universal Studio. In 1940, Allan Jones left MGM, stating that "all good singing roles seemed to go to Nelson Eddy." He went to Paramount and then signed a contract with Universal. When Universal announced a new talking version of *The Phantom of the Opera,* Jones hoped he would get the romantic lead, especially since he was under contract. Nelson Eddy was at liberty, was offered the role, and once again "the good singing role went to Nelson Eddy." Years later, Nelson remarked that he never watched his old movies, nor was he too proud of most of them. But, of all the films he did make, *The Phantom of the Opera* was his favorite role.

The following year, he starred in a mediocre screen version of the Maxwell Anderson-Kurt Weill musical, *Knickerbocker Holiday.* Ultimately, in 1946, his voice was used to good effect for the cartoon character Willie, singing "The Whale Who Wanted to Sing at the Met" in Walt Disney's *Make Mine Music.* Finally, in 1947, in conjunction with Herbert J. Yates and Republic Pictures, he made his final screen appearance in the film *Northwest Outpost,* originally entitled *End of the Rainbow.* (The film was shown in Europe under its original title). For the third time, Ilona Massey was his co-star and the first-rate supporting cast included Joseph Schildkraut, Elsa Lanchester and Hugo Haas. Despite an excellent Rudolf Friml score, lavish production values and first-rate play-dates, *Northwest Outpost* remained fairly remote.

Nelson continued to devote his time to concert work and recordings. Like his famous co-star Jeanette MacDonald, Nelson entered the recording industry through his films. After the release of *Naughty Marietta,* Nelson became a popular musical star, and there were thousands of requests for his recordings. To comply, RCA Victor signed him to a short-term contract. Nelson made his first commercial recording on March 11, 1935. Like Jeanette, they were recordings of his movie hit songs. In Nelson's case they were "I'm Falling in Love with Someone" backed with "Tramp, Tramp, Tramp Along the Highway" and "Ah, Sweet Mystery of Life" (solo) backed with " 'Neath the Southern Moon." In 1938, Nelson signed a long-term contract with Columbia Records, with whom he remained until 1957. His first recordings at Columbia were four Indian love lyrics, "The Temple Bells" backed with "Less Than the Dust" and "Kashmiri Song" ("Pale Hands I Love") backed with "Till I Wake." In 1957, for RCA Victor once again, he recorded a new album with Jeanette MacDonald and four "night" songs. He then signed an exclusive contract with Everest Records, where first release was an album of duets with Gale Sherwood, including numbers from their night club act. Over the years, Nelson recorded some 284 songs and some twenty-five albums. One of his most popular recordings was "Short'nin' Bread," first recorded on February 1, 1942. Nelson was joshed mercilessly by Charlie McCarthy on the radio about this song—but it soon became a popular trademark for him.

Nelson's concerts continued until 1952. At these concerts, his favorite and most popular, pieces were "The Lord's Prayer," "The Trumpets Shall Sound," from Handel's *Messiah* and the Figaro aria from *The Barber of Seville.* But his more than receptive audiences were never satisfied until he climaxed each appearance with encores of songs from his films made with Jeanette MacDonald.

Nelson's television debut was on the "Alan Young Show" on October 11, 1951. The show was such a success that Nelson was asked to appear again the following week. This was the start of many TV appearances over the years; "The Ed Sullivan Show," "What's My Line," "The Big Record," and guest shots with Dinah Shore, Rosemary Clooney, Bob Hope, Danny Thomas, Tennessee Ernie Ford, Jack Paar, Mike Douglas, Merv Griffin, Pete Potter, and others. Most memorable was the Max Liebman Spectacular Special of *The Desert Song,* a full-length version co-starring Nel-

Entertaining troops at Teheran

With Dorothy Kirsten on
the "Kraft Music Hall" radio show

With Salvatore Baccaloni in a scene from "The Desert Song" TV Special on NBC in 1955

son and Gale Sherwood with Otto Kruger, Rod Alexander and Bambi Lynn.

In 1952, Nelson came to a decision. He chose to leave the concert stage and become a night club headliner. After auditioning many female singers, he finally chose Gale Sherwood as a partner. Miss Sherwood, a lovely blonde, hailed from Hamilton, Ontario, and moved to Hollywood with her family in 1939. She appeared in several motion pictures, the most notable being *Song of my Heart*, a Hollywood biography of Tchaikovsky. Nelson made his night club debut in 1953 at Tops, San Diego, California. Gale Sherwood first appeared with Nelson in Las Vegas, Nevada, shortly thereafter. For the next fifteen years he was one of the most successful entertainers, playing the best supper clubs in the United States, Canada, Mexico, and Australia. So popular was Nelson's night club act, that upon his death in 1967, he had bookings two years in advance. At the time, there was talk that Allan Jones would honor some of the engagements, but this never materialized.

In Nelson's last interview, shortly before his death, he said, "I'm working harder that I ever have in my life." And when questioned about his Hollywood days, he added: "I never miss those years now. Today I'm enjoying life. I've got a home, a wife, a whole new set of friends, and I make more money in nightclubs than I did in movies. Singing is what I've always wanted to do. I'm no romantic, but I've done a few things people have enjoyed and remembered. I wasn't wonderful, just an ordinary man taking part in a picture. I'm a talent, I never had a loud enough or high enough voice to be an operatic baritone."

On Sunday evening, March 5, 1967, while appearing at the Sans Souci Hotel in Hollywood, Florida, Nelson suffered a stroke. Gale Sherwood had left the stage. She and Nelson had just finished singing "Love and Marriage." Nelson, ready to go onto his next number, faltered. He turned to Ted Paxton, his accompanist for thirty nine years, and said, "Will you play 'Dardanella', maybe I'll get the words back," making a joke at the last. He then asked the audience if there was a doctor in the house. Before an enthusiastic audience of over 400, he was helped offstage by his two partners, Gale and Ted, where a doctor from the audience administered first aid. He was rushed to Mt. Sinai Hospital in Miami, Florida, where he died twelve hours later on March 6, 1967.

The funeral was a private Episcopal service, with only family, close friends and a few fans present. It was conducted by the Reverend J. Herbert Smith, Rector of All Saints Church in Beverly Hills, California. Nelson's close friend, Z. Wayne Griffin, gave the eulogy. Among those who attended Nelson's services were Wayne Griffin, Gene Raymond, Dr. Rex Kennemer, Delmer Daves, Henry Dreyfuss, Bob Breckner, Meredith Willson, Art Rush, Bronislav Mlynarski, Lloyd Nolan and Ted Paxson.

With Gale Sherwood toasting their successful engagement at New York's Empire Room, in the Waldorf Astoria, in January 1960

Mrs. Eddy was accompanied by her son, Sidney Franklin, Jr. and his wife; four grandchildren; her sister and her family; nieces and their families; Nelson's nephews, Wayne Linton Brown and Elliott Eddy Brown; Gale Sherwood; Wendy Paterson; Mildred Hudson (Nelson's secretary); Myron Hanly; Mrs. Robert Breckner (Nelson's cousin Sally); Mrs. Lloyd Nolan; Mrs. Arthur Rush; Mrs. Bronislav Mylnarski (actress, Doris Kenyon); Elinor Remmick Warren (Mrs. Z. Wayne Griffin); Mrs. Ted Paxson; Mr. E. J. Osborne; Bob Hunter; Mrs. Meredith Willson; Thomas Freebairn-Smith; Harper MacKay; Robert Armbruster; Rosemary Sullivan; Lucille Mereto; Valerie Davison; and several close members of the Nelson Eddy International Music Club.

Holding a copy of the sheet music for "Indian Love Call" from *Rose Marie* 26 years after the film premiered

SWEETHEARTS

The Great
Jeanette MacDonald-Nelson Eddy Feud

For years, in magazines, newspapers, and radio and television talk shows people have stated and argued that Jeanette MacDonald and Nelson Eddy really never got along. I hope this book ends forever this great misconception about two fine artists.

Jeanette MacDonald and Nelson Eddy were both very professional people, but each approached their film careers in an entirely different manner. Jeanette was very proud of her film career, and she approached it with the same seriousness as she did her concert and opera work. Nelson, on the other hand, was never fond of his film career and approached it with a much lighter attitude. Consequently, on the set, Nelson and Jeanette did not always agree as to the degree of effort each star should put into his or her role. This would, at times, lead to some disagreement on the set. Jeanette would worry about and check out costumes, make-up, cameramen, camera angles and most phases of the total film product. Nelson would learn his lines, go to costume, then to make-up, then onto the set, do a scene, and then forget about it. Like any two people who live together or work together and are spending a great deal of time with each other, there were moments of total disagreement. But, that did not make them dislike or hate each other! In fact, it increased their respect for each other. Each knew the other's differing outlook on a career and each admired the other for it.

The press, learning of these on-the-set differences, thought they would make good copy and elaborated on them. Some of Jeanette and Nelson's films had scenes where the stars were supposed to be arguing. The press thought they saw more than acting in some of these scenes. This can be best explained in Nelson's own words. On October 20, 1959, Nelson appeared on the "Tonight Show," the television program then hosted by Jack Paar. In reply to Jack's remark, "The other rumors were that you didn't get along, that you two didn't like each other," Nelson said, "Oh, I know what you're talking about now. I know how it started, 'The MacDonald-Eddy Feud.' You've heard about that one . . . well, it's a lot of baloney, if I'm allowed to use such a word on this network. In most of our picture, *Sweethearts*, we were lovey-dovey, but we had one scene where we had an argument. We were on stage doing a scene and I upstaged her and she upstaged me, and we were snarling at each other and everything. I stepped on her dress and she stepped on my foot—just kinda looked real. We were acting very well in those days! There was a reporter for a newspaper syndicate who saw this and he said, 'It's true. You can see it right there. They're trying to upstage each other and get the best of each other.' And he wrote a big piece in the paper, ran a column and a half, the big MacDonald-Eddy feud! They went and they said, 'No, pal, look this is the picture. It's supposed to be that way. They are having a little fight, and later they make up and everything is fine, and you'll see it when the picture comes out.' He says, 'All right, I'll wait.' Well, it just so happened that they cut out the scene! So, now he knows

ROSE MARIE

Off-camera during filming of *Rose Marie*

GIRL OF THE GOLDEN WEST

he's right and it gets all over. What're you gonna do? I love her . . . I think she loves me!''

The main source of the supposed feud came from the rivalry between the Jeanette MacDonald and Nelson Eddy Fan Clubs, and the feud still continues to this day. Jeanette had two fan clubs. The first and original was started in 1930. It was a fan club for Jeanette MacDonald and Maurice Chevalier. Its president was Miss Pearl Katzmann and its headquarters were in New York. By 1934, it had become The Original Jeanette MacDonald Fan Club with its club journals entitled ''Musical Echoes.'' It disbanded in 1965 upon Jeanette's death. The president at that time was Glenna Riley, of New Castle, Indiana, who had been president for thirty-three years. The other Jeanette MacDonald Fan Club was started in 1938 by Miss Mary Miller. It then became incorporated with a club of Miss Alma Calligan's, to become The International Jeanette Mac-Donald Fan Club, a club still in existence today with over 600 members. It is very ably run by its devoted and dedicated president, Miss Clara Rhoades of Topeka, Kansas. It is the largest fan club in the world for a star who has been dead for more than 10 years. It continues its club publication, entitled ''The Golden Comet.''

The Nelson Eddy Music Club was established in 1935, with its first president being Miss Loretta Schultz. The club's journals were entitled ''The Shooting Star.'' The club disbanded in 1967 upon Nelson's death. Its president was Mrs. Thelma Cohen, of Little Neck, New York, who had held the position for twenty-six years. The club was later reinstated under the leadership of Mr. Perry Pickering of Baltimore, Maryland. During the height of the stars' popularity, their fan clubs had great power and received much attention from the press and radio. While many fans admired both stars equally, many felt the one star infringed upon the other's potential. The fan clubs soon started their own ''wars'' between each other. If Jeanette got more close-ups in one film (yes, they actually counted them), Nelson's fan club was up in arms. If Nelson got to sing one song more, even one note more, than Jeanette, her fan club would rebel. And so it continued. Much of this discontent covered by the press and radio was originally perpetuated by the stars' fan clubs. Even today, at showings of the stars' co-starring films, members of one's fan club will try to applaud louder or longer than the other's.

Through the years, Jeanette and Nelson remained good friends although not necessarily close ones. Several things accounted for this. Jeanette and Gene Raymond were very social people and entertained quite frequently with their friends. They attended many social functions throughout their life together. Nelson, on the other hand, kept very much to himself. He and his wife only entertained at small dinner parties in their home and were very seldom seen socializing in Hollywood. Jeanette and Nelson's lifestyles were far apart. Jeanette saw Allan Jones and his wife Irene Hervey more frequently than she did Nelson. Knowing of Nelson and Ann Eddy's preference for small dinner parties, they were invited to many such dinners at Twin Gables, the Raymond's Tudor home in Beverly Hills.

Nelson started his night club tour in 1953 and it took him all over the country and to foreign shores. Very often, he was away from his California home and did not see his wife, much less friends. Jeanette did comparatively little traveling during the last ten years of her life because of her health. However, whenever Nelson played Los Angeles or New York City, and Jeanette was in town at that time, she always made a point to see Nelson's act on opening night. Nelson's conflicting nightclub dates never let him attend any of Jeanette's summer stock performances, but he always sent her a congratulatory telegram on opening night.

In her will, Jeanette left her private print of *Rose Marie* to Nelson Eddy. Gene Raymond, remembering that Nelson had shared so many fond memories with Jeanette, asked Nelson to be an honorary pallbearer at Jeanette's funeral. Ann Eddy, knowing the great loss Gene Raymond felt and his loneliness since Jeanette's death, and now faced with this same loss, asked Mr. Raymond to be pallbearer at Nelson's funeral. These certainly were not the acts of people who disliked each other. These were the acts, thoughts, and feelings of two people who were generally fond of each other, respected each other, and had the great admiration for each other's talent.

From 1935 to 1942, Jeanette MacDonald and Nelson Eddy were lovers on the screen, enthralling millions of fans with their make-believe love. From 1935 up until their deaths, Jeanette MacDonald and Nelson Eddy were two individual people, living individual lives, yet drawn together by their mutual respect and admiration for each other. And, through this association the world's two most perfectly blended voices thrilled the world with the romance of music.

Letters From Friends of Jeanette and Nelson

JOAN CRAWFORD

Philip dear,

Thank you for your nice letter. I am happy to know that your book is progressing so well. . . .

Jeanette and Nelson were completely dedicated to their craft and to music, which they loved. There was a special chemistry and friendship between them that the world shared, and that blend made their co-starring films outstanding entertainment and great successes at the box office.

I remember Nelson as an earnest man, eager to please, and grateful for the opportunity to be in "The Dancing Lady," which I believed was his first film. He was startlingly handsome with a beautiful baritone voice. Jeanette, with her beauty, grace, and charm, and her equally lovely soprano voice, was a delightful foil for him.

They were greatly loved by the public and by all of us who worked with them and knew each of them personally.

Bless you, and my best wishes to you. . . .

As ever,
JOAN

My first recollection of Jeanette MacDonald and Nelson Eddy was in Hungary and Vienna. When I was a music student there, I would save my lunch money so that I could see them in films like, *Naughty Marietta, Rose Marie,* etc. To me they were the most talented and beautiful artists of our time. Little did I dream those days, that I would see them in person, and that I should be the partner of Nelson for three films, "Rosalie," "Balalaika," and "Northwest Outpost." Nelson was a great singer and a great person. He was always a great help to me while filming. When he sang to me, he made sure that my face was toward the cameras. He told me, "you are new, they must see you." He was both generous and modest in his greatness. MGM publicity department tried to create jealousy between Miss MacDonald and me, saying, "Ilona Massey is a singing Garbo. Miss MacDonald had better look out." Miss MacDonald did not have to look out for anyone. She had talent and beauty that was unique; she was also a lady in the truest sense of the word. Even now, when I have the opportunity, I see their films with nostalgia, for that era of loveliness has left us. I feel sorry for the now generation. They are void of illusion and the naked truth is sad. What can they look forward to? They have seen and tasted all. I am fortunate to have known Jeanette and Nelson. They have given much to this world and the world loved them. It would be a better world today, if their living beauty and voices could inspire the now generation.

God be with them for eternity.

ILONA MASSEY

Altogether I was in the supporting cast of four of Jeanette and Nelson's musical films: *Rose Marie, I Married An Angel,* and *Cairo,* without Nelson, and *Rosalie,* without Jeanette. All four films were directed by W.S. Van Dyke. Woody had the reputation of being the speediest director on the MGM lot, in fact he spent twice the time on retakes then on the original shooting script. *Rose Marie* was a very big hit. Nelson looked extremely handsome as a Mountie and Jeanette a very lovely Marie de Flor. I remember Jeanette always as a very gracious and lovely woman, and it was always a pleasure to play a scene with her, for she was an accomplished actress and devoted to her profession—a perfectionist. She was happily married to Gene Raymond, a very handsome actor indeed and a very good friend. Nelson was a completely charming man, simple and unassuming. He was the kindest human being around. Both Jeanette and Nelson were two super stars. They were attractive persons with pleasing personalities and wonderful voices and for almost ten years their films made box office history. I lost two wonderful friends and they are always in my prayers.

REGINALD OWEN

Jeanette MacDonald and Nelson Eddy were my fellow musicians as well as my close friends. They had certain personal characteristics in common, which involved almost story-book qualities; unremitting fealty to their profession, loyalty to their associates, and "no compromises" in the matter of doing justice to their talents. Unflaggingly did they accept the virtually unlimited demands their careers constantly made upon them. Their particular niche in show business annals is secure for all time to come.

MEREDITH WILLSON

I worked with Jeanette and Nelson for many years. They were gracious and most cooperative. They were beautiful people.

KAY MULVEY

RALPH EDWARDS

Dear Mr. Castanza:

I knew Jeanette MacDonald and Gene Raymond better than I knew Nelson Eddy. I think my only meeting with Nelson Eddy was in connection with the "This is Your Life" presentation I conducted with Jeanette MacDonald as the principal subject. We held Nelson for the surprise finale of her life story, telling of the wedding of Jeanette and Gene. Over the speakers we heard the voice of Nelson Eddy singing "Oh,

Perfect Love." It was the song Nelson sang at Jeanette's and Gene's wedding and, of course, we had Nelson backstage.

. . . .Helen Ferguson, Jeanette's long time friend and public relations adviser, had brought Jeanette to the El Capitan Theatre on Vine Street in Hollywood, on the pretext that she was going to present an award to me from the Optimists Club of California. She did not know at that time that it was just an excuse to get her in the theatre so we could reveal her story and present people from her past to her. Poor Helen Ferguson almost passed out from shock when, in parking her car, Jeanette pointed to an automobile nearby and said, "For heaven's sake, there's Nelson's car. What on earth do you suppose it's doing here?"

Helen made some remark like, "Oh, I think he's rehearsing for that thing down the street," and kept walking right in. Fortunately, our producer, Axel Gruenberg, was at the door to immediately take Jeanette in hand and explain about the "award" to me at the beginning of the program.

It was only our seventh "This is Your Life" show and the subjects were not so tuned in to the element of surprise on which our show puts so much emphasis. . . .

At any rate, in the turning of the spotlight on Jeanette and the excitement of the surprises that followed, Jeanette had completely forgotten about Nelson Eddy's automobile in the parking lot until she heard "Oh, Perfect Love" and the unmistakable voice that sang it. Nelson's appearance was a perfect ending to a half-hour I shall always remember. Jeanette MacDonald's life was a rare and wonderful existence. We presented to her a sailor she jitterbugged with at the Hollywood Canteen, Verle Cowling, of Huntington Beach, California; her seventh grade English teacher at Dunlap School in Philadelphia, Miss Edna Clear, of Ocean City, New Jersey; Dr. Willsie Martin, minister of the Wilshire Methodist Church in Los Angeles, who performed the marriage of Jeanette and Gene; her first singing teacher, Grace Adele Newell, who said she told Jeanette, "If you can take the work and sacrifice, no galavanting, no smoking, no drinking, you will be a great singer some day." I must say that Jeanette apparently took Miss Newell's advice. In all the years I knew Jeanette, I never saw her smoke or drink.

Also present were her sisters Blossom—the actress, Marie Blake—and Elsie, who taught Jeanette her first songs when, at the age of three, Jeanette made her debut as a singer at the Tennant Memorial Presbyterian Church, at 52nd and Arch Street, Philadelphia, at a church social. Elsie accompanied her at the piano at that time.

We pulled another surprise on Jeanette during the show. Gene was in New York—or at least Jeanette thought so. We called him on the phone and heard him say, "I'm watching the show here in New York. You look wonderful, honey, and I'll call you as soon as it's over." You can imagine Jeanette's

added surprise when, in explaining that she and Gene arrived at the same time at the door of a house where they were invited to a party, everyone there assumed they knew each other — I said, "Well then, Jeanette, actually you and your husband never have been formally introduced. After fifteen years of married life, I think it's time you two were introduced to each other. Mrs. Gene Raymond, I would like to have you meet Mr. Gene Raymond," and Gene walked onstage.

All the magic of Jeanette's life—from Shillings Ice Cream Parlor in Philadelphia, through *Maytime* and *The New Moon* motion pictures with Nelson Eddy, *San Francisco* with Clark Gable, *Bittersweet*, *The Girl of the Golden West*, *Sweethearts*, *Naughty Marietta* and *Rose Marie* also with Nelson Eddy, *The Love Parade* with Maurice Chevalier, *The Vagabond King* with Dennis King, *Monte Carlo, One Hour With You*, and *Love Me Tonight*, her story book marriage to the wonderful Gene Raymond, the lonely year from Gene while he was fighting for our country overseas and she visited Army camps, donated her $96,462.80 profit from 12 concerts to the Army Emergency Relief Fund—all this went through my mind as I sat at the service for Jeanette at her all-too-young passing in 1965.

I recall the fact that her father, who died in 1924, never saw his celebrated daughter become a star and I felt a certain sadness that this was, in effect, a final curtain for a great lady and a great star. I went back to my office and did something I had never done before and never did after— I called the Metromedia TV station in Los Angeles KTTV, and asked George Putnam if he would like to run a condensed version of the "This is Your Life" story of Jeanette MacDonald, made several years earlier. He was delighted and I appeared on the newscast personally that night in a rare replay of one of our over 400 "This is Your Life" subjects. On the way out of the studio I was paged to the phone. It was Gene Raymond, whose permission we had obtained for the reprise of the story. "Thanks, Ralph," Gene said, "for Jeanette and me...."

RALPH

The Films

The Love Parade

A Paramount Picture   1929

Executive Producer, Adolph Zukor. Produced and directed by Ernst Lubitsch. Screenplay by Ernest Vadja and Guy Bolton; based on *The Prince Consort* by Leon Xanrof and Jules Chancel. Photography by Victor Milner. Orchestrations and musical arrangements by Victor Schertzinger and the Paramount Music Department. Art direction and set decoration supervised by Hans Dreier. Film cutter, Merrill White.   150 minutes.

Songs   "Dream Lover," "My Love Parade," "March of the Grenadiers," "Anything to Please the Queen," "Let's Be Common," "Paris Stays the Same," "Nobody's Using It Now," "Ooo La La," and "The Queen Is Always Right." Music by Victor Schertzinger. Lyrics by Clifford Gray.

CAST

Count Alfred, MAURICE CHEVALIER; *Louise, Queen of Sylvania,* JEANETTE MacDONALD; *Jacques, the Valet,* Lupino Lane; *Lulu, Queen's Maid,* Lillian Roth; *Master of Ceremonies,* Edgar Norton; *Prime Minister,* Lionel Belmore; *Foreign Minister,* Albert Roccardi; *Admiral,* Carleton Stockdale; *Minister of War,* Eugene Pallette; *Afghan Ambassador,* Russel Powell; *First Lady in Waiting,* Margaret Fealy; *Second Lady in Waiting,* Virginia Bruce; *Extra,* Jean Harlow.

SYNOPSIS

Much to the despair of her cabinet members, Queen Louise rules her kingdom of Sylvania with a lonely heart until Count Alfred, her foreign emissary, returns from Paris in disgrace. After reading a detailed report of the count's escapades, the queen sends for him and asks him to demonstrate his prowess as a great lover. His exhibition is so effective, the queen marries him.

Count Alfred is soon balking at taking orders from his wife although he keeps up appearances because he knows the queen is trying to negotiate a loan from a foreign power. But when she orders him to attend the opening of

With Ethel Griffies (center), Virginia Bruce (left) and Margaret Fealy (right)

With Lionel Belmore and Maurice Chevalier

the royal opera, he refuses. In despair, the queen goes alone. And her sudden joy, when he does show up, is shortlived because the count tells her he intends leaving in the morning for Paris, where he will seek a divorce.

Late that night the queen comes to his rooms for the first time and implores him to stay. But until she promises to allow him to become king as well as her husband, he remains adamant. Once she capitulates, they embrace and live happily ever after.

With Virginia Bruce and Margaret Fealy

COMMENTS

The Love Parade, Jeanette MacDonald's film debut, and also Ernst Lubitsch's debut as a director of sound films, was also Maurice Chevalier's first satisfying film since arriving in the United States two years earlier. Jeanette made a stunning and thoroughly captivating queen. She had an innate sense of humor fitting nicely into the character of the queen, who after all was still a woman at heart. Her voice registers nicely both in song and in the spoken line.

Photoplay

Sparkling as Burgundy, and almost as intoxicating, *The Love Parade* is one of the outstanding pictures of the year. It is Lubitsch's most brilliant effort since *The Marriage Circle.* The little director here conquers light opera. Jeanette MacDonald is an eye-feast as the queen and sings well.

Rob Wagner's Script

Of course Lubitsch had magnificent paints, but then he always chooses his colors with intelligence. Chevalier is without a doubt one of the most charming personalities that has come to the screen, a fine comedian and a polished actor. Jeanette MacDonald is also a finished artist, sings well, and is beautiful when her face is illuminated by laughter, but rather cold and hard in repose.

(Left) Singing "The March of the Grenadiers"

With Dennis King

The Vagabond King

A Paramount Picture   1930

Produced by Adolph Zukor. Directed by Ludwig Berger.
Screenplay by Herman Mankiewicz; based on the play *If I
Were King* by Justin Huntly McCarthy; based on the Op-
eretta, *The Vagabond King* by William H. Post, Rudolf
Friml and Brian Hooker. Photography by Henry Gerrand
and Ray Rennahan. Technicolor Consultant Natalie Kal-
mus. Recording directors, Ben Adams and Charles Foster.
Recording engineer, Franklin Hansen. Costumes by
Travis Banton. Film editor, Merrill White.   104 min-
utes.

Songs "Huguette Waltz," "Love for Sale," "Love Me
Tonight," "Only a Rose," "Some Day," "Song of the
Vagabonds," "If I Were King," "King Louie," and
"Mary, Queen of Heaven." Music and lyrics by Rudolf
Friml, Brian Hooker, Leo Robin, Sam Coslow, and Newell
Chase.

CAST

Francois Villon, DENNIS KING; *Katherine*, JEANETTE
MacDONALD; *Louis XI*, O.P. Heggie; *Huguette*, Lillian
Roth; *Thibault*, Warner Oland; *Olivier*, Arthur Stone;
Astrologer, Thomas Ricketts.

SYNOPSIS

Paris is besieged by the army of the rebellious Duke of
Burgundy, and the vacillating King Louis XI is helpless,
because his own Grand Marshall is dealing secretly with
the Burgundians. The Paris rabble, led by the poet Francois Villon, and his wench Huguette, sings ribald, insult-
ing songs about the king. Villon saves the Lady Katherine,
niece to King Louis, from the mob, and falls in love with
her. Villon kills the villainous treacherous ex-marshall at a
fete where an attempt is made to abduct the king.
Huguette gives her life protecting Villon, and Villon leads
the Paris mob against the Burgundians and defeats them.

With Dennis King and O. P. Heggie

COMMENTS

"The Vagabond King" has been done in many versions. In 1911, Selig Productions did a one reel silent movie. In 1920, Fox Films produced a silent version "If I Were King" which starred William Farnum. In 1925, Dennis King, Carolyn Thomas and Jane Carroll starred on Broadway in a musical version of "The Vagabond King." In 1927, United Artists based a screenplay by Paul Bern, "The Beloved Rogue" on "If I Were King" and starring John Barrymore in the lead role. In 1934, Jeanette played the lead role in a "Lux Radio Theatre" presentation. In 1936, "Lux Radio Theatre" did a repeat engagement that starred John Boles and Evelyn Venable. In 1938, Paramount did "If I Were King" a nonmusical directed by Frank Lloyd, starring Ronald Colman, Basil Rathbone, Frances Dee, and Ellen Drew in the lead roles. In 1944, again "Lux Radio Theatre" did a presentation of "The Vagabond King" which featured Kathryn Grayson and Dennis Morgan. This was twelve years before Kathryn Grayson appeared in the second movie version. In 1956, Paramount offered a third musical version of "The Vagabond King" with Kathryn Grayson and Oreste in the lead roles. Michael Curtiz directed. Victor Young composed additional songs for this one.

Weekly Variety

Jeanette MacDonald, featured, is extremely beautiful in the clinging satins of the period. Her performance supplies the requisite aroma of glamour. . . . In all departments of actual production, "The Vagabond King" is top-notch costume picture. What it lacks is comedy and consistency, it makes up in strong or unusual sequences, great photography and general splendor.

With Dennis King

Paramount On Parade
A Paramount Picture   1930

Produced by Albert A. Kaufman. Production supervisor, Elsie Janis. Directed by Dorothy Arzner, Otto Brower, Edmund Goulding, Victor Heerman, Edwin H. Knopf, Rowland V. Lee, Ernst Lubitsch, Lothar Mendes, Victor Schertzinger, Edward Sutherland, Frank Tuttle. Photography by Victor Milner and Harry Fischbeck. Production design by John Wenger. Choreography by David Bennett. Film editor, Merrill White. In some sequences, color by Technicolor.   101 minutes.

Songs   "My Marine," music and lyrics by Ray Egan and Richard Whiting. "I'm In Training for You," "Drink to the Girl of My Dreams," and "Dancing to Save My Soul" by L. Wolfe Gilbert and Abel Baer. "I'm True to the Navy Now," "Paramount On Parade" and "Anytime Is the Time to Fall In Love" by Elsie Janis and Jack King. "All I Want Is Just One" by Leo Robin and Richard Whiting. "Sweeping the Clouds Away" by Sam Coslow.

CAST
The following personalities appeared in the English, Spanish, French, German, Japanese, Swedish, or Spanish speaking versions:
RICHARD ARLEN, JEAN ARTHUR, WILLIAM AUSTIN, GEORGE BANCROFT, CLARA BOW, EVELYN BRENT, MARY BRIAN, CLIVE BROOK, VIRGINIA BRUCE, NANCY CARROLL, RUTH CHATTERTON, MAURICE CHEVALIER, GARY COOPER, LEON ERROL, STUART ERWIN, KAY FRANCIS, SKEETS GALLAGHER, HARRY GREEN, MITZI GREEN, JAMES HALL, PHILLIPS HOLMES, HELEN KANE, DENNIS KING, ABE LYMAN, JEANETTE MacDONALD, FREDRIC MARCH, NINO MARTINI, MITZI MAYFAIR, DAVID NEWELL, JACK OAKIE, WARNER OLAND, ZELMA O'NEAL, EUGENE PALLETTE, JOAN PEERS, WILLIAM POWELL, CHARLES "BUDDY" ROGERS, LILLIAN ROTH, JACKIE SEARL, STANLEY SMITH and FAY WRAY.

With David Newell and unidentified player

Jack Oakie, Mary Brian, Gary Cooper

SYNOPSIS
The best of the twenty revue numbers that have been featured in the English-speaking version were utilized in the Spanish version, along with a new format in which Jeanette MacDonald served as Mistress of Ceremonies, introducing the various acts and describing them in the Spanish language. Jeanette was also the star of one classic song number set in Venice. It had Jeanette and David Newell floating in a gondola along the Grand Canal.

COMMENTS
Jeanette's musical number was to have been her only appearance in the English version. However, in the final print, her number was completely cut out. Today, the only appearance of Jeanette available is in several Spanish version prints. One was shown as recently as 1960 in Mexico City. All other film of her are lost and her name never appears neither on any print credits, nor in any reviews of the film.

Time

"This is one of those elaborate miscellanies with which the big production companies utilize the spare time of the stars on contract to them. It is an unusually good one . . . rapid, handsome, brightened with flashes of wit probably put in by Elsie Janis, who supervised it."

With Kay Francis and Jack Oakie

Let's Go Native

A Paramount Picture   1930

Executive producer, Adolph Zukor. Produced and directed by Leo McCarey. Original screenplay by George Marion, Jr. and Percy Heath. Photography by Victor Milner. Dances and ensembles staged by David Bennett. Recording engineer, Harry O. Mills.   63 minutes.

Songs "I've Got a Yen for You," "It Seems to Be Spring," "Let's Go Native," "My Mad Moment," "Don't I Do," "Pampa Rose," and "Joe Jazz." Music and lyrics by George Marion, Jr. and Richard Whiting.

CAST
Joan Wood, JEANETTE MacDONALD; *Voltaire McGinnis,* JACK OAKIE; *Wally Wendell,* JAMES HALL; *Jerry,* SKEETS GALLAGHER; *Constance Cooke,* KAY FRANCIS; *Basil Pistol,* William Austin; *Chief Officer Williams,* David Newell; *Wallace Wendell, Sr.,* Charles Sellon; *Creditor's Man,* Eugene Pallette.

SYNOPSIS
Millionaire Wallace Wendell threatens to disinherit his son, Wally, Jr., if he doesn't marry the daughter of the head of a rival soap firm. Undaunted, Wally sails for Buenos Aires, working as a stoker alongside Voltaire McGinnis, an on-the-lam cab-driver who was forced to leave the U.S. or face the financial consequences of an auto accident. Wally's fiancee, Joan Wood, is also aboard, a passenger traveling deluxe class although she is broke and hoping to get financial backing for a show she intends opening in Buenos Aires. A shipwreck casts everybody on a tropical isle, dominated by Jerry, a onetime hoofer who has taught the natives how to sing and dance. Wally falls for Joan who comes into possession of the island by buying off the natives with the costumes intended for her show. When Wallace, Sr. arrives with a rescue party, Wally's

marriage to Joan is sanctioned and Wendell, Sr. buys the island, rich in pearls and oil, from her. But after the deal is finalized, an earthquake occurs and the island sinks into the ocean.

With Jack Oakie, James Hall and William Austin

COMMENTS

The story of *Let's Go Native* reminds one of *The Admirable Crichton,* a property Paramount had filmed four times previously, including a Cecil B. DeMille version called *Male And Female.* It was filmed again as *We're Not Dressing,* more faithful to the original, and three other versions, including an English production. This was the only film in which Kay Francis sang on screen in her own voice.

The New York Times

In spite of hilarious moments of good slapstick, and deft spontaneous playing of Jack Oakie, this is the kind of picture that disappoints it's makers and audiences because neither can figure out why it isn't funnier. The trouble really is that it is a comedy built around a comic situation. That is a dramatic fallacy.

With Skeets Gallagher

The Lottery Bride

An Artcinema Associates, Inc. Production Released by United Artists   1929

Produced by Arthur Hammerstein. Directed by Paul Stein. Original story, Herbert Stothart. Continuity by Howard Emmett Rogers. Adaptation by Horace Jackson. Photographed in Two-Color Technicolor by Ray June. Musical arrangements by Hugo Riesenfeld. Musical conductor, Herbert Stothart. Art direction and production design by William Cameron Menzies and Park French. Costumes by Alice O'Neill. Edited by Robert J. Kern.   80 minutes.

Songs   "You're an Angel," "I'll Follow the Trail," and "My Northern Light." Music by Rudolph Friml. Lyrics by J. Kerin Brennan. Additional Song: "High And Low." Music and lyrics by Carter Desmond, Howard Dietz, and Arthur Schwartz.

CAST

Jennie, JEANETTE MacDONALD; *Chris,* JOHN GARRICK; *Hoke,* JOE E. BROWN; *Hilda,* ZaSu PITTS; *Olaf,* Robert Chisolm; *Alberto,* Joseph Macaulay; *Boris,* Harry Gribbon; *Nels,* Carroll Nye.

SYNOPSIS

Against her fiancé Chris' wishes, Jennie enters a marathon dance contest with hopes that winning first prize will help her brother, Nels, replace money he has taken from the bank that employs him. But before this happens, the police appear to arrest Nels, and Jennie, because she helps him escape, is herself arrested. Meanwhile, Chris leaves the country, unaware of Jennie's incarceration.

On the day she is released from prison with her spirit broken, Jennie is greeted by her friends Hilda and Hoke and learns she has been offered a solution to her problem by a mining camp matrimonial agent: being sent to the mines as a potential lottery bride for one of the workers.

With Robert Chisholm

With ZaSu Pitts and Joe E. Brown

With Robert Chisholm, Carroll Nye and John Garrick

COMMENTS

The Lottery Bride represented Arthur Hammerstein's first (and last) venture as a film producer. His material might have been the basis of an entertaining operetta but the silly screenplay nullified much of the story's validity. Friml composed one of his second drawer scores, but the music remained the film's high point. Lavish production design by William Cameron Menzies was dissipated by garish colors . . . pinks and greens being predominant. And in the breaking up of an ice block, the papier-mâché ice floes showed brown when the snow was scuffed.

The New York Times

Rudolf Friml's musical compositions in *The Lottery Bride*, Arthur Hammerstein's audible screen production are thoroughly enjoyable, but like most operettas, the story, the dialogue and, to some extent, the acting are quite another matter. It is a pictorial contribution that causes one to wish that the performers would sing more and talk considerably less. The principals in this film are Jeanette MacDonald, John Garrick, Joseph Macaulay, Robert Chisholm and Joe E. Brown. The first four are responsible for the rendition of the engaging ballads and Mr. Brown looks after the comedy, which he does extraordinarily well. Hence, during the exhibition of this picture one may appreciate the melodies and laugh and chuckle at the fun.

With Jack Buchanan

Monte Carlo
A Paramount Picture   1930

Produced by Adolph Zukor. Associate producer and director Ernst Lubitsch. Screenplay by Ernest Vajda; from the play, *The Blue Coast,* by Hans Muller and Episodes from *Monsieur Beaucaire* by Booth Tarkington and Evelyn Sutherland. Additional dialogue by Vincent Lawrence. Photography by Victor Milner. Sets by Hans Dreier. Sound recording engineer, Harry D. Mills. Costumes by Travis Banton. Film editor, Merrill White.   90 minutes.

Songs "Give Me a Moment Please," "Beyond the Blue Horizon," "This Is Something New to Me," "Women Just Women," "I'm a Simple-Hearted Man," "She'll Love Me and Like It," "Whatever It Is, It's Grand," "Always In All Ways," "Trimmin' The Women," and "Day of Days."

Music by Richard Whiting and Frank Harling. Lyrics by Leo Robin.

CAST
Count Rudolph Falliere, JACK BUCHANAN; *Countess Vera von Conti,* JEANETTE MacDONALD; *Maria,* ZaSu Pitts; *Armand,* Tyler Brook; *Prince Otto von Seibenehim,* Claude Allister; *Duke Gustavo von Seibenehim,* Edgar Norton; *Paul,* John Roche; *Master Of Ceremonies,* Albert Conti; *Lady Mary,* Helen Garden; *Monsieur Beaucaire,* Donald Novie; *Harold,* David Percy; *Lord Windorset,* Erik Bey.

With Jack Buchanan

With Claude Allister

SYNOPSIS

Countess Vera von Conti flees by train from her husband-to-be Prince Otto von Seibenehim. She is down to her last ten thousand francs when she checks in at Monte Carlo. Count Rudolph Fallieres is dazzled by the Countess' beauty when he sees her enter the gambling casino, and persuades her that his caressing her hair will bring her luck at the gambling tables. Countess Vera prospers and hires Fallieres as her hairdresser, not knowing his true station in life. Fallieres soon becomes not only her hairdresser, but her personal servant and chauffeur; he also secretly loves her and phones her every night to pour out his love in song, to which she is soon tempted to answer lyrically. The Countess Vera, about to be forced by financial reasons to wed the stuffy Duke, is annoyed by Fallieres, and dismisses him. But at the opera where Monsieur Beaucaire is being performed, the Countess spies Fallieres in another box and suddenly realizes that Fallieres, like Beaucaire, is no servant at all but a man of nobility and considerable wealth. The lovers are thus reunited.

COMMENTS

Monte Carlo represented Lubitsch at the peak of his talent. It was witty, sophisticated, and loaded with continental charm. Jeanette again played a temperamental lady of the world. It was one of her most deliciously amusing portrayals and she also was in excellent voice. Jack Buchanan, a legendary British musical comedy star, was superb as the nobleman-cum-hairdresser. Mr. Buchanan, who made his American film debut in a Warner musical, *Paris,* did not appear in another major American film until the MGM success *The Band Wagon* in 1953.

Variety

Miss MacDonald was the illumination. She played well all of the time, at moments exceptionally, as in the bit with Buchanan, where she feared he would be nabbed by other women. Miss MacDonald's singing is also most acceptable. As a matter of record, she steals the picture, besides being an A-1 looker.

Film Daily

Coming through again with the ultimate in finesse that has made him a master hand in polished screen entertainment, Ernst Lubitsch turns out another of his highly delectable comedies with song. It is smart piece that swings along to the tune of steady and keen enjoyment.... Miss MacDonald is a treat again.

Oh, For a Man

A Fox Picture   1930

Executive producer, William Fox. Associate producer and director, Hamilton McFadden. Screenplay by Lynn Starling and Philip Klein; based on the story *Stolen Thunder* by Mary F. Watkins. Photography by Charles Clarke. Recording engineer, E. Clayton Ward. Costumes by Sophie Wachner. Film editor, Al DeGaetano.   78 minutes.

Song "I'm Just Nuts About You. Music and lyrics by William Kernell.

CAST

Carlotta Manson, JEANETTE MacDONALD; *Barney McGann,* REGINALD DENNY; *Totsy Franklin,* Marjorie White; *Pug Morini,* Warren Hymer; *Laura,* Alison Skipworth; *Peck,* Albert Conti; *Frescatti,* Bela Lugosi; *Costello,* Andre Cheron; *Kerry Stokes,* William B. Davidson.

SYNOPSIS

Carlotta Manson, opera star, is disgusted with her own boring personal life, and threatens to forsake opera for a romantic fling. Barney McGann, a second-story man from Third Avenue, steals into her boudoir one night to make away with her jewels, but Carlotta awakens and is fascinated by the burglar. They marry, but in her villa in Italy, Barney fed up with being husband to a diva, returns to Third Avenue. Carlotta, disconsolate, returns to opera. She is revisited via the second-story route by her estranged husband, and confesses that her heart belongs to him and that she still loves him. Barney, realizing he is needed, remains.

COMMENTS

The story of *Oh, For a Man* originally appeared in the *Saturday Evening Post* in June 1930. Reginald Denny plays a successful burglar, so successful he escapes retribution in the end. This was before the new production code went into effect and was, therefore, permissable. But because of Denny's character, Fox *could not* reissue the film, as they had planned to do, after MacDonald's later popularity because of code rulings. While Jeanette was filming, *Oh, For a Man* Nelson was busy with his concert tours.

With Reginald Denny

With Alison Skipworth

Photoplay

One of the brightest, without a doubt. . . the story of a grand opera star who marries a burglar. A farcical notion which comes off because of its excellent treatment by Director Hamilton MacFadden and the merry acting of Jeanette MacDonald and Reginald Denny in the leads. Nice work also by Warren Hymer, Alison Skipworth and Marjorie White. A worthy winner.

Motion Picture

A load of laughs, which makes it well worth a boost. *Oh, For a Man,* is not big, but is amusing and sexy in a manner which can prove offensive to nobody . . . Miss MacDonald exhibits a versatility that has not appeared in her earlier work. She gives an extremely good performance.

Don't Bet on Women

A Fox Picture   1931

Produced by William Fox. Directed by William K. Howard. Screenplay by Lynn Startling and Leon Gordon; based on the story *All Women Are Bad* by William Anthony McGuire. Photoplay by Lucien Andriot. Recording by Albert Protzman. Film editor, Harold Schuster.   70 minutes.

CAST

Roger Fallon, EDMUND LOWE; *Jeanne Drake,* JEANETTE MacDONALD; *Herbert Drake,* ROLAND YOUNG; *Tallulah Hope,* UNA MERKEL; *Chipley Duff,* J.M. Kerrigan; *Doris Brent,* Helene Millard; *Butterfield,* Henry Kolker.

SYNOPSIS

Roger Fallon has become a woman-hater, after his experience in both marraige and love affairs, and is of the opinion that the entire female sex is rotten to the core and cannot be trusted. At a big gathering, Herbert Drake happily wed to a beautiful woman, tells Fallon he's wrong and bets him $10,000 that the next woman entering the room will not let Fallon kiss her within 48 hours. The next woman entering the room turns out to be Drake's own wife, and Jeanne and Drake and Fallon are stuck with the bet. Jeanne Drake chances to learn of the wager and determines to teach both her husband and the woman-hating Fallon a lesson about women. She does so, but in the process nearly falls for Fallon, and he for her.

COMMENTS

Jeanette played the heroine charmingly, but she was wasted in a songless role. The film achieved a quiet popularity as the second feature in its neighborhood runs. The national distribution benefited from a well publicized premiere at New York's prestigious Roxy Theatre.

With Una Merkel and Roland Young

With Edmund Lowe and Roland Young

The New York Times

An excellent comedy sketch, bubbling with bright lines and originality. It's plot may be trifling, but it is worked out with real skill and directed imaginatively by William K. Howard.

With Sally Blane and Joyce Compton

With Roland Young

Annabelle's Affairs

A Fox Picture   1931

Executive producer, William Fox. Associate producer, William Goetz. Directed by Alfred Werker. Screenplay by Leon Gordon; based on the play *Good Gracious Annabelle* by Clare Kummer. Photography by Charles Clarke. Sound engineer, Albert Bruzlin. Costumes by Sophie Wachner. Film editor, Margaret Clancy.   76 minutes.

Song "If Someone Should Kiss You." Music and lyrics by James Hanley.

CAST

John Rawson, VICTOR McLAGLEN; *Annabelle Leigh,* JEANETTE MacDONALD; *Roland Wimbledon,* ROLAND YOUNG; *James Ludgate,* SAM HARDY; *Wickham,* William Collier, Sr.; *Lottie,* Ruth Warren; *Mabel,* Joyce Compton; *Dora,* Sally Blane.

With Ruth Warren

SYNOPSIS

Annabelle Leigh, married only eleven hours to escape being compromised, is given stock in a rich mining enterprise by her husband and cautioned never to part with the investment. Her newlywed husband and she then separate. Annabelle's extravagances force her to pledge the shares for a loan she makes, and so the stock falls into the hands of her husband's millionaire rival. Aware that her husband, whom she barely knows by sight, is returning to her, Annabelle poses as a cook and obtains employment in the millionaire's home, hoping to get her hands on the stock. Her husband returns, shaves off his beard, and obtains employment from his rival as a yacht captain. Annabelle not only gets the stock back, but falls in love with the man she had married.

COMMENTS

Good Gracious Annabelle, a comedy in 3 acts, opened at the Republic Theatre, New York City on October 31, 1916 and ran 111 performances. It was produced and staged by Arthur Hopkins with Lola Fisher starring as Annabelle. Roland Young was also in the cast as Wilbur Jennings, a minor character (he later married playwright Clare Kummer's daughter, Marjorie). Clare Kummer, nee Beecher, was descended from both Henry Ward Beecher and Harriet Beecher Stowe, author of *Uncle Tom's Cabin.* The first *Good Gracious Annabelle* film was released by Paramount in 1918 and starred Billie Burke. Jeanette's song in the film is well sung and spotted in the action.

With William Collier, Sr., and Victor McLaglen

Motion Picture Herald

Jeanette MacDonald's performance is thoroughly delightful. Her sense of comedy is fine and her place among the screen's leading comedians seems assured. She has only one song, the rendition of which is nicely performed.

With Maurice Chevalier

One Hour With You
A Paramount Picture   1932

Produced and Directed by Ernst Lubitsch and George Cukor. Screenplay by Samson Raphaelson; based on the play *Nur ein Traum* by Lothar Schmidt (Goldschmidt). Photography by Victor Milner. Set decorations by Hans Dreier. Gowns by Travis Banton. Film cutter William Shay.   80 minutes.

Songs "One Hour With You," "Oh, That Mitzi!," "We Will Always Be Sweethearts," "What Would You Do," "Three Times A Day," and "What a Thing Like a Wedding Ring Can Do." Music by Oscar Straus. Lyrics by Leo Robin. Interpolated music by Richard Whiting.

CAST
Dr. Andre Bertier, MAURICE CHEVALIER; *Colette Bertier*, JEANETTE MacDONALD; *Mitzi Olivier*, GENEVIEVE TOBIN; *Adolphe*, CHARLES RUGGLES; *Professor Olivier*, ROLAND YOUNG; *Mlle. Martel*, Josephine Dunn; *Detective*, Richard Carle; *Marcel*, Charles Coleman; *Policeman*, Charles Judels; *Police Commissioner*, George Barbier; *Mitzi's Maid*, Barbara Leonard; *Colette's Maids*, Sheila Mannors and Leonie Pray; *Taxi Driver*, George David.

With Genevieve Tobin

With unidentified player in a scene from the French version

With Charles Ruggles

SYNOPSIS

After three years of marriage, Dr. Andre Bertier, and his wife Colette, are still so much in love that when they embrace in the Bois de Boulogne, the local gendarme, not believing they're married, advises them to retire to the privacy of a boudoir. They do so, and there Dr. Bertier takes the audience into his confidence about his marital happiness. Mitzi Olivier, Colette's best friend, is attracted by the doctor and pays a professional call on him. Dr. Bertier is eventually compromised and named in a divorce suit by Mitzi's husband, a history professor, but he finally persuades Colette that he is absolutely innocent, and they stay together, in love.

COMMENTS

This film was a remake with music of Ernst Lubitsch's 1924 Warner Bros film *The Marriage Circle,* which starred Florence Vidor, Monte Blue, Marie Prevost, Creighton Hale and Adolphe Menjou. The film was co-directed by Lubitsch and George Cukor. Cukor started it when Lubitsch took over as production supervisor of all Paramount pictures but after he completed *Broken Lullaby* (*The Man I Killed*) he began making suggestions to Cukor, who was not in accord. Consequently Cukor quit, Lubitsch finished the film and took sole credit. A Director's Guild arbitrator and a court ruling restored Cukor to full co-directorship although, by that time, the film had been released. Originally Carole Lombard and Kay Francis were to have co-starred but ultimately they were replaced by MacDonald and Tobin.

The New York Times

Maurice Chevalier is as enjoyable as ever. There is his smile and also his stare— a stare of discomfort when he is dumbfounded. But whether he is solemn or laughing, he is always engaging. Miss MacDonald is charming as Colette.

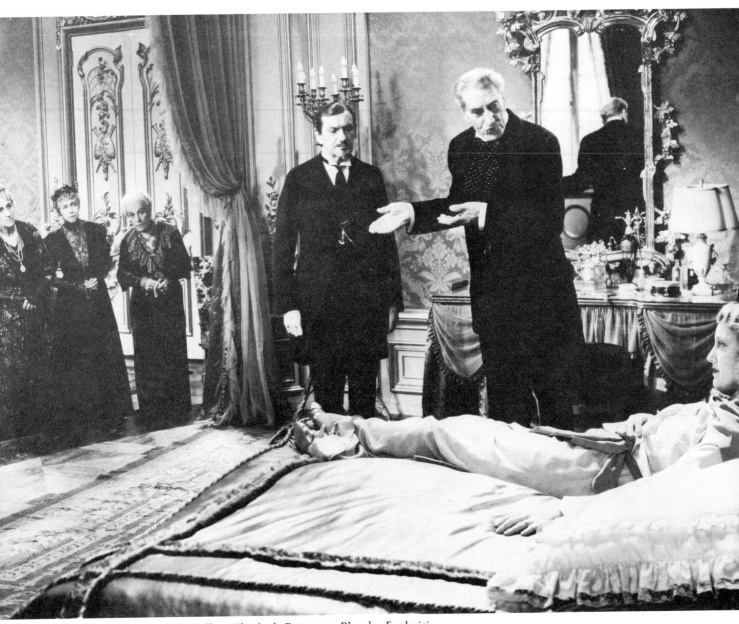

With Ethel Griffies, Elizabeth Patterson, Blanche Frederici,
Joseph Cawthorn and C. Aubrey Smith

96

With Maurice Chevalier

Love Me Tonight
A Paramount Picture   1932

Produced and directed by Rouben Mamoulian. Screenplay by Samuel Hoffenstein, Waldemar Young, and George Marion, Jr.; based on an uncompleted play by Leopold Marchand and Paul Arment. Photography by Victor Milner. Sound recording, M.M. Paggie. Art director, Hans Dreier. Film editor, Rouben Mamoulian. Film cutter, William Shay.   90 minutes.

Songs "Isn't It Romantic," "Mimi," "Love Me Tonight," "Poor Apache," "Lover," "The Song of Paree," "How Are You," "A Woman Needs Something Like That," and "The Son of a Gun Is Nothing But a Tailor." Music by Richard Rodgers. Lyrics by Lorenz Hart.

CAST

Maurice Courtrelin, MAURICE CHEVALIER; *Princess Jeanette*, JEANETTE MacDONALD; *Vicomte de Vareze*, Charles Ruggles; *Count de Savignac*, Charles Butterworth; *The Duke*, C. Aubrey Smith; *Countess Valentine*, Myrna Loy; *First Aunt*, Elizabeth Patterson; *Second Aunt*, Ethel Griffies; *Third Aunt*, Blanche Frederici; *The Doctor*, Joseph Cawthorn; *Major Domo*, Robert Greig; *Emile*, Bert Roach; *Laundress*, Cecil Cunningham; *Dressmaker*, Ethel Wales; *Valet*, Edgar Norton; *Groom*, Herbert Mundin; *Shirtmaker*, Clarence Wilson; *Composer*, Tyler Brooke, *Bakery Girl*, Marion "Peanuts" Byron; *Pierre*, George Daris; *Taxi Driver*, Rolf Sedan; *Hat Maker*, Tony Merlo; *Boot Maker*, William H. Turner; *Grocer*, George "Gabby" Hayes; *Chef*, George Humbert.

SYNOPSIS

Maurice Courtelin, a happy-go lucky Parisian tailor, goes to a great castle on a provincial estate to collect a bill run up by the Vicomte de Vareze, scion of a noble family. To save face since he cannot pay the bill, the Vicomte introduces Maurice as a Baron, and he's royally accepted. This subterfuge is used to allow the Vicomte time to convince the Duke, who holds a tight hand on the family purse, that he is not a profligate philanderer as suspected.

Princess Jeanette, a haughty member of the noble family who had previously encountered and snubbed Maurice, falls in love with him when he's considered a nobleman. When his true state is revealed, she first rejects him, but then goes forth in romantic pursuit.

COMMENTS

Of all Jeanette's pre-Nelson films, this was her best and is still considered one of the great original screen musicals. Jeanette's singing of "Lover" and Chevalier's "Mimi" are charming renditions included in the story. Mamoulian disliked Jeanette so thoroughly that a few reviewers felt Myrna Loy, in a much less important role, seemed more romantically right for Chevalier than Jeanette. But, Jeanette worked harder and better against such odds and came out with her best screen work to date. Mamoulian developed a two page idea for a play into the screenplay but had Rodgers and Hart write the songs before the script was completed. The dialogue and situation were written around music and lyrics rather than the standard way of shoehorning songs in a libretto.

Variety

Treatment takes on the color of a musical comedy frolic, whimsical in it's aim and deliciously carried out in it's pattern, in it's playing and in it's direction. Effect is altogether delightful. Gives Miss MacDonald an excellent opportunity for quiet comedy playing, which she rises charmingly to meet.

Photoplay

What a picture. First, you have Chevalier (and last, you have Chevalier, and all through this riot entertainment you have Chevalier). And adding her beauty and lovely voice, you have that delightful Jeanette MacDonald.

With Myrna Loy and Maurice Chevalier

With Charles Butterworth

99

Broadway to Hollywood

A Metro-Goldwyn-Mayer Picture   1933

Associate producer, Harry Rapf. Directed by Willard Mack. Screenplay by Willard Mack and Edgar Allan Woolf. Photography by William Daniels and Norbert Brodine. Musical arrangements, Dr. William Axt. Art direction by Stanwood Rogers. Film editors, William S. Gray and Ben Lewis.

Songs "We Are the Hacketts" music and lyrics by Al Goodhart; "When Old New York Was Young,'" music and lyrics by Howard Johnson and Gus Edwards; "Ma Blushin Rosie," music and lyrics by Edgar Smith and John Stromberg; "Come Down Ma Evenin Star,": music and lyrics by Robert B. Smith and John Stromberg; and "In the Garden of My Heart" music by Ernest Ball, lyrics by Caro Roma.

CAST

Lulu Hackett, ALICE BRADY; *Ted Hackett,* FRANK MORGAN; *Anne Ainslee,* Madge Evans; *Ted Hackett, Jr.,* Russell Hardie; *Ted Hackett, Jr.* (as a child), Jackie Cooper; *Ted the Third,* Eddie Quillan; *Ted the Third* (as a child), Mickey Rooney; *David,* Tad Alexander; *Joe Mannion,* Edward Brophy; *Wanda,* Ruth Channing; *Grace,* Jean Howard. AND: Jimmy Durante, Nelson Eddy, Fay Templeton, May Robson, Claire DuBrey, Muriel Evans, Claude King, Una Merkel and Albertina Rasch Dancers (all in very brief bits).

SYNOPSIS

The story deals with three generations of the vaudeville trouping Hackett family. In the 1880s down at Tony Pastor's on 14th Street, Ted and Lulu Hackett are headliners, but their act goes downhill when Lulu takes time out to give birth to their son, Ted Jr. In a few years, however, the son steps into the scene and onto the stage, and lifts the Hacketts back into top booking. He goes with Weber and Fields, and Ted and Lulu find themselves once more on the downgrade. Ted, Jr. marries a pretty dancer, Anne Ainslee, but abandons her for liquor and women. After the birth of her son, Anne commits suicide. Ted, Jr. goes off to fight in World War I where he is killed in action. The two older Hacketts attempt a comeback with their grandson Ted III, who gets a Hollywood contract. Ted III is nearly

Frank Morgan, Alice Brady and Tenen Holtz

detoured into the same downward path that destroyed his own father, but he reforms. When the big scene of his musical is being filmed, his grandparents are on the set watching. Grandfather Hackett has a heart attack and dies, and Lulu bravely, in the tradition of "the show must go on," does not spoil the big musical take.

COMMENTS

Nelson Eddy's role consisted of little more than a cameo bit when, as an entertainer, he sang, "In the Garden of My Heart." William A. Brady, Alice Brady's father, was among the many who helped launch Nelson on a singing career in his early concerts. Alice Brady and Nelson were friends when he made his small contribution to this film.

The New York Times

Five years ago, MGM made an expensive music-comedy called *The March of Time* (no connection with Time, Inc.'s radio March of Time), decided it was not worth releasing but a shade too good to shelve. After endless ineffective tinkering, Willard Mack and Edgar Allan Woolf rewrote the story. MGM selected a new cast. *Broadway To Hollywood* is the result. The few remaining shots from the old film—a Technicolor ballet executing a blurred march down an exaggerated stairway—might better have been left out.

Variety

A saga of the theatre that will please. It should get fair box office attention and, in the more sophisticated show centers, appeal unusually to the behind-the-footlights fans.

With Joan Crawford

Dancing Lady

A Metro-Goldwyn-Mayer Picture   1933

Produced by David O. Selznick. Directed by Robert Z. Leonard. Screenplay by Allen Rivkin and P.J. Wolfson; based on the novel by James Warner Bellah. Photography by Oliver T. Marsh. Musical conductor, Lou Silvers. Dances by Sammy Lee and Eddie Prinz. Special Effects by Slavko Vorkapich. Sound recording engineer, Gavin Burns. Art and set decorations by Cedric Gibbons and Harry Oliver. Costumes by Adrian. Film editor, Margaret Booth.   94 minutes.

Songs   "My Dancing Lady," music and lyrics by Dorothy Fields and Jimmy McHugh; "Everything I Have Is Yours," "Let's Go Bavarian," and "Heigh-Ho the Gangs All Here" music and lyrics by Harold Adamson and Burton Lane; "Rhythm of the Day" music and lyrics by Richard Rodgers and Lorenz Hart.

CAST

Janie, JOAN CRAWFORD; *Patch Gallagher,* CLARK GABLE; *Tod Newton,* FRANCHOT TONE; *Himself,* Fred Astaire; *Mrs. Newton,* May Robson; *Rosette,* Winnie Lightner; *Ward King,* Robert Benchley; *Steve,* Ted Healy; *Vivian Warner,* Gloria Foy; *Art,* Art Jarrett, *Bradley, Sr.,* Grant Mitchell; *Bradley, Jr.* Maynard Holmes; *Themselves,* The Three Stooges, Moe Howard, Jerry Howard and Larry Fine; *Arthur,* Sterling Holloway; *Himself,* NELSON EDDY.

SYNOPSIS

Janie works in burlesque but is aiming for the Broadway musical stage. Ted Newton, a rich playboy, is enamored of Janie, but she is lukewarm toward him. Determined to win Janie through fair means or foul, Tod offers her both marriage and a job in the chorus of a Broadway musical he happens to be backing. Janie accepts the job in the chorus, but demurs at marrying him. Finally she promises she will become Mrs. Newton if the show is a flop. Tod sets out to sabotage the production to make sure she will marry him, adopting a host of ingenious methods in the process. But Tod is up against Patch Gallagher, the show's hard-boiled dance director, who is determined to make the production a success. Patch and Janie do not hit it off at first. He feels she has been forced on him because of her connections with Tod, and he harasses her in front of the rest of the cast. But she surmounts the humiliations Patch purposely inflicts and convinces him in time she is a talented performer. Finally, when Tod's machinations have almost succeeded, and it looks like the show won't go on, Janie and Patch, who are gradually falling in love, band together and manage to open. Janie's singing and dancing are the hit of the show, Tod realizes Janie loves Patch, and Patch and Janie clinch for the fadeout.

COMMENTS

This backstage story was very well done. Joan Crawford, Clark Gable, and Franchot Tone turned in excellent performances. This film also served as Fred Astaire's movie debut. From the concert stage, making his screen debut in a specialty number was the singing baritone, Nelson Eddy. Both Mr. Eddy and Mr. Astaire went on to box-office stardom for the next two decades.

Time

The versatile Mr. Gable is surprisingly cast as a stage director, instead of a gangster, and might make hoofing the rage. Perhaps the film should have been called *Dancing Man* to introduce the new Clark Gable. Although it would be a premature observation to say that Fred Astaire may have some future competition from Gable, it would not be invalid.

With Ramon Novarro

The Cat and the Fiddle
A Metro-Goldwyn-Mayer Picture   1934

Produced by Bernard Hyman. Directed by William K. Howard. Screenplay by Sam and Bella Spewack; based on the stage play by Jerome Kern and Otto Harbach. Photography by Harold Rosson and Charles Clarke. Musical direction by Herbert Stothart. Recording director, James Brock. Art director, Theodore Toluboff. Set decorations, Edwin B. Willis. Costumes, Adrian. Film editor, Frank Hull.   90 minutes.

Songs "The Night Was Made for Love," "Try to Forget," "She Didn't Say Yes," "One Moment Alone," "A New Love Is Old," "I Watched the Love Parade," "Poor Pierrot." Music by Jerome Kern. Lyrics by Otto Harbach.

CAST
Victor RAMON NOVARRO; *Shirley*, JEANETTE Mac-DONALD; *Daudet*, FRANK MORGAN; *Charles*, Charles Butterworth; *Professor*, Jean Hersholt; *Odette*, Vivienne Segal; *Theatre Owner*, Frank Conroy; *Taxi Driver*, Henry Armetta; *Concierge*, Andrienne D'Ambricourt; *Rudy*, Joseph Cawthorn.

SYNOPSIS
Escaping from an irate restaurant proprietor in Brussels, Victor Florescu hops into a a taxi that happens to be occupied by Shirley Sheridan, just arriving from New York to study music from Victor's professor. Instead of complying with her angry demands to get out of the cab, Victor makes love to her brazenly but charmingly. She is going to the pension next to his own, he demands that she go to his. In the struggle over her baggage, Shirley's clothing is scattered on the sidewalk and she dashes angrily into her pension. As Victor is unable to pay the fare, the driver takes his music, his only valuable possession. The night before Victor's operetta, *The Cat and the Fiddle*, is to open the producer-husband of the leading lady, who has been financing the show, finds his wife with her arms around the reluctant Victor. He withdraws his support and drags his wife out of the theatre. Victor gives a worthless check to keep the theatre open, but the leading man and the orchestra also desert him. In desperation to keep out of jail, Victor decides to play the lead himself. Charles goes to Shirley, who is about to marry Daudet, and pleads with her to save Victor, since she knows the part. She turns him down, so he appears at the theatre with a wheezy prima donna, who proceeds to get drunk after the curtain goes up

With Charles Butterworth, Leonid Kinskey and Ramon Navarro.

With Frank Morgan, Ramon Novarro and Jean Hersholt

for the first act. Victor, in his dressing room, is frantic. He is about ready to call off the performance when he hears Shirley's voice from the stage, singing the part. Unbelieving, he rushes to the wings; it is Shirley. When the curtain goes down for the act he begs her to come back to him. She coldly declares she appeared to play the part to save him from jail. He continues wooing and in the third act, dramatically, while the music swells, she surrenders to his hungry arms. The love scene continues after the curtain is down.

COMMENTS

This was Jeanette's first film under her new MGM contract, though she took second billing to Ramon Novarro. Louis B. Mayer signed her with intentions of starring her in *I Married an Angel*. The Hays Office thought the script too risque. The property was shelved until 1942, when it served as the last picture for the MacDonald-Eddy combination. Jeanette had her first costumes designed by Adrian. However, her costume worn in the finale operetta sequence was designed for and used by Joan Crawford in the "In Barbarian" number in *Dancing Lady* (1933). For the grand finale of the operetta sequence, the number was filmed in the new three-color process of Technicolor.

Variety

For better or worse the original *The Cat and the Fiddle* stage script has been altered by the film adapters so that the only thing of merit remaining is the music. The Spe-
wacks substituted light comedy for the original's more serious mood. Result isn't strong entertainment, but the music, production excellence and the combination of Ramon Novarro and Jeanette MacDonald as a singing team in the picture and a co-starring pair for the billing should insure fair or better returns. . . . For the closing production number, in which lovers' reunion is spotted, the picture goes color. The highly colored photography is flattering to Miss MacDonald, but Novarro looks better in plain black and white. As to the picture, the change in color in the last few feet doesn't help much, since the picture is over by then, and nothing can make much difference.

Screenland

This picture has Rhythm. Not only Jerome Kern's tunes but William K. Howard's direction carries out the idea; rippling along with all the gay charm of a Kern melody. "The Night Was Made For Love" and this picture was made for the sparkling personalities of Jeanette MacDonald and Ramon Novarro. It's a happy merger of music, and talents. Ramon will win you completely as the impulsive and ardent young music student . . . or you're the one who didn't like *The Three Little Pigs*. And when Ramon pursues the lovely Miss MacDonald all over Brussels and finally to Paris and back to Brussels again . . . I hope you'll be running right along. I know I was. Jeanette's voice and looks match . . . both enchanting. Novarro sings too, and nicely . . . and his ingratiating boyishness disarms all criticism of this Mexican Peter Pan.

Student Tour

A Metro-Goldwyn-Mayer Picture   1934

Produced by Monta Bell. Directed by Charles "Chuck" Reisner. Screenplay by Ralph Spence and Philip Dunne. Original story by George Seaton, Arthur Bloch, and Samuel Marx. Photography by Joseph Valentine. Musical direction by Jack Virgil. Choregraphy by Chester Hale. Film editor, Frank Hull.   80 minutes.

Songs   "I Say It with Music," music and lyrics by Jimmy Durante; "A New Moon Is Over My Shoulder," "Snake Dance," "By the Taj Mahal," "From Now On," and "Fight Em," "The Carlo," music and lyrics by Nacio Herb Brown and Arthur Freed.

CAST

Hank, JIMMY DURANTE; *Lippy,* CHARLES BUTTERWORTH; *Ann,* MAXINE DOYLE; *Bobby,* PHIL REGAN; *Lilith,* Florine McKinney; *Mushy,* Douglas Fowley; *Jeff,* Monte Blue; *Cayenne,* Betty Grable; *Mary Lou,* Fay McKenzie; *Himself,* Nelson Eddy; *Hercules,* Herman Brix; *Dance Team,* Florence and Alvarez.

SYNOPSIS

Although the boating crew of Barlett College have all flunked their grades in philosophy, they won the regatta, which would entitle them to participate in a world cruise were their grades satisfactory. To allow them to make the tour, the assistant coach convinces the philosophy professor that his ugly duckling daughter will attract a beau among the athletes during the cruise. The ugly duckling daughter makes small headway during the trip, which includes a visit to China and India where the collegians stage a water carnival in the pool that rests in front of the Taj Mahal. In England, their last stop, the ugly duckling emerges, without her glasses, at a celebration dance and wins the heart of one of the athletes.

Florine McKinney, Jimmy Durante, Charles Butterworth and Betty Grable

COMMENTS

A highlight of *Student Tour* was the marvelous singing of "The Carlo" by Nelson. The song has a thunderous beat and sound which becomes very exciting. It is definitely a song to which only a voice like Eddy's could do full justice. Betty Grable and Herman Brix, who later changed his name to Bruce Bennett, appeared in minor roles. While Nelson was filming *Student Tour* Jeanette had returned from her European concert tour and immediately signed a long term contract with Metro-Goldwyn-Mayer Pictures.

Photoplay

The priceless nonsense of Charles Butterworth and Jimmy Durante, the new combination of Phil Regan and Maxine Doyle, and the novel idea of using a floating college for a musical background, makes this refreshing entertainment. Butterworth is a professor of philosophy and Durante an athletic trainer. Nelson Eddy's marvelous singing climaxes the story.

With Maurice Chevalier

The Merry Widow
A Metro-Goldwyn-Mayer Picture   1934

La Veuve Joyeuse
A Metro-Goldwyn-Mayer Picture   1934

Executive producer, Irving Thalberg. Associate to Mr. Thalberg, Henry W. Savage. Produced and directed by Ernst Lubitsch. Screenplay by Ernest Vajda and Samson Raphaelson; based on Franz Lehar's operetta *The Merry Widow*. Libretto and lyrics by Victor Leon and Leo Stein. Photographed by Oliver T. Marsh. Music by Franz Lehar. Additional music by Richard Rodgers. Lyrics by Lorenz Hart and Gus Kahn. Music adapted, arranged, orchestrated and conducted by Herbert Stothart. Sound recording engineer, Douglas Shearer. Art direction and set decoration by Cedric Gibbons, Gabriel Scognamillo, Frederic Hope and Edwin B. Willis. Choreography by Albertina Rasch. Gowns by Adrian. Men's Costumes by Ali Hubert. Edited by Frances Marsh (under the supervision of Ernst Lubitsch). Filmed at MGM's Culver City Studio.   110 minutes.*

Songs "Girls, Girls, Girls," "Widows Are Gay," "I'm Going to Maxim's," "Vilia," "Tonight Will Teach Me to Forget," "The Merry Widow Waltz," and "Melody of Laughter" (instrumental).

* The English language version of *The Merry Widow*, available for national bookings since 1962 as one of the MGM Library of "Golden Operetta" series, runs 103 minutes.

A simultaneously produced French language version of *The Merry Widow*, directed by Ernst Lubitsch with a screenplay translated by Marcel Archard and French Lyrics by Andre Herrnez. Maurice Chevalier and Jeanette MacDonald recreated their original roles but Akim Tamiroff, also in the English language version, played *Turk* in this production. Other production credits are substantially the same for this version as the English language production with the exceptions noted above and with these cast replacements: Marcel Vallee, Mme. Daniele Parola, Andre Berley, Fifi D'Orsay, Pauline Garon, George Davis, Jean Perry, Albert Petit, Emil Dellys, Georges Renavent, Georgette Rhodes, Anita Pike, Odette Duval, Lya Lys, George Nardelli, Constant Franke, Jacques Venaire, George Renault, Marcel Venture, Fred Cravens, Sam Ash, Harry Lamont, George de Gombert, Arthur de Ravenne, Fred Malatesta, George Colega, Adrienne d'Ambricourt, Eugene Borden, Jules Raucort, Andre Cheron, Eugene Beday, Juliet Dika, Carry Daumery, August Tollaire, Gene Gouldeni, Jacques Lory, Andre Ferrier.   114 minutes.

With Mina Gombell

CAST (English Language Version)

Danilo, MAURICE CHEVALIER; *Sonia,* JEANETTE MacDONALD; *Ambassador,* Edward Everett Horton; *Queen,* Una Merkel; *King,* George Barbier; *Marcele,* Minna Gombell; *Lulu,* Ruth Channing; *Orderly,* Sterling Holloway; *Turk,* Henry Armetta; *Maid,* Barbara Leonard; *Valet,* Donald Meek; *Manager of Maxim's,* Akim Tamiroff; *Zizipoff,* Herman Bing; *Adamovitch,* Lucien Prival; *Sonia's Maids,* Luana Walters, Sheila Mannors, Caryl Lincoln, Edna Waldron, Lona Andre; *Maxim's Girls,* Patricia Farley, Shirley Chambers (Ross), Maria Troubetskoy, Eleanor Hunt, Jean Hart, Dorothy Wilson, Barbara Barondess, Dorothy Granger, Jill Bennett, Mary Jane Halsey, Peggy Watts, Dorothy Dehn and Connie Lamont; *Escorts,* Charles Requa, George Lewis, Tyler Brookes, John Merkyl, and Cosmo Kyrle Bellew; *Waiters,* Gino Corrado and Perry Ivins; *Prisoner,* Kathleen Burke; *Ambassador,* George Baxter; *Dancer,* Paul Ellis; *Shepherd,* Leonid Kinskey; *Newspaper Woman,* Evelyn Selbie; *Lackey,* Wedgewood Nowell; *Defense Attorney,* Richard Carle; *Prosecuting Attorney,* Morgan Wallace; *Judge,* Frank Sheridan; *Doorman,* Arthur Byron; *Wardrobe Mistress,* Claudia Coleman; *Excited Chinaman,* Lee Tin; *Animal Woman,* Nora Cecil; *Orthodox Priest,* Tom Frances; *Nondescript Priest,* Winter Hall; *Newsboy,* Matty Rupert; *Fat Lackeys,* Dewey Robinson, Russel Powell, and Billy Gilbert; *Drunks,* Arthur Housman and Johnny "Skins" Miller; *Gypsy Leader,* Hector Sarno; *Violinist,* Jan Rubini; *Arresting Officer,* Jason Robards, Sr.; *Headwaiter,* Albert Pollet; *Gabrielovitsch,* Rolf Sedan; *Goatman,* Jacques Lory.

With Edward Everett Horton and Maurice Chevalier

With Maurice Chevalier

SYNOPSIS

The year is 1885. In Marshovia, a Central European Kingdom, so small that it is just a spot on the map, it is the custom for widows to go about heavily veiled during their period of mourning. This custom, followed by a wealthy young widow named Sonia, is tantalizing to Captain Danilo who would very much like to see what she looks like. He has the audacity to climb the wall of her garden in an effort to make her acquaintance, but she snubs him and refuses to be interested. Sonia hasn't forgotten Danilo, and out of curiosity follows him to Maxim's, where she is mistaken for one of the light ladies who frequent the cafe. Unaware of her true identity, Danilo becomes interested and takes her up to a private dining room, but is piqued when she resists his advances. Waltzing with him, she leaves him in disgust. Convicted of treason, he is sent to prison. Deciding that Sonia's money is lost to Marshovia and that his kingdom will be bankrupt, the king is helping the queen pack in preparation for departure, when word comes that Sonia has gone to visit Danilo in prison. The King orders Sonia to be locked in the cell with Danilo. The lovers decide they are not going to be tricked into reconciliation, but love conquers in spite of their resolutions and a minister, sent down to the prison by the king, marries them through a peephole in the door of the cell.

COMMENTS

Franz Lehar's operetta had been a stage perennial for several decades when, in 1924, Erich Von Stroheim saw its potential as a silent film and starred Mae Murray and John Gilbert in the lead roles.

In 1933, Maurice Chevalier signed a contract with MGM. The previous year they had managed to lure Jeanette to their studio and away from Paramount where she, more or less, had merely been a leading lady whose name headed the supporting casts of Chevalier films. Jeanette's first starring role for MGM was in *The Cat And The Fiddle,* which she carried off with great style. It was her performance in *The Merry Widow* that proved to Irving Thalberg and Louis B. Mayer that they had not made a mistake. Her potential as a money-making personality was extraordinary. When Chevalier was assigned to do a sound re-make of *The Merry Widow* he was delighted. He wanted Grace Moore for his leading lady. Miss Moore, however, had already made two previous films for MGM, *New Moon* and *A Lady's Morals,* and each was a financial fiasco. Somewhat to Chevalier's annoyance he again found himself working with Jeanette. He considered her something of a prude and a hypocrite.

The Merry Widow was Jeanette's best film since *Love Me Tonight*. She sang with a verve that had not always been apparent in some of her earlier films, and she proved herself to be both beautiful and a beguiling romantic. Almost simultaneously she could display an insouciant air of beguilement while retaining an aura of mystery and glamour which is really the essential image of all great feminine stars of the sound film. Jeanette had the further advantage of stage training and a vibrant soprano voice, which appealed to the average filmgoer who had never seen a live operetta but who was enchanted by Jeanette's singing style. Often on the screen, when her characterization and performance appeared somewhat aloof, her musical moments were always an occasion when she and her audience shared an intimacy that emanated it's own kind of rapture. Jeanette had not only perfected the ideal rapport with audiences, she also perfected the ideal style for herself in duets, and never again during her entire screen career did she sing against a song lyric.

The two versions she did of *The Merry Widow* are both memorable experiences and it is something of a pity that the French language production isn't available for audiences to see and compare with the English version. Jeanette's true versatility is most notable when you realize the subtle ways in which she altered a voice inflection or a song lyric to suit a French or an English song. Years later in 1952 MGM released a new version of *The Merry Widow* which was an even more lavish production than the two 1934 productions. It added the lure of Technicolor. Unfortunately, that's all it had. This production presented us with Lana Turner, lushly photographed, impeccably gowned. Miss Turner used what looked like a cavalcade of lessons in what not to do in a musical fantasy. She had merely to watch a single screening of the Jeanette MacDonald version to know how that role can be successfully played.

Weekly Variety

In his leads, Lubitsch picked a double plum out of the talent grab bag. Maurice Chevalier and Jeanette MacDonald both are aces as Danilo and Sonia. The former Paramount pair once again works beautifully in harness, with this one a cinch to enhance Miss MacDonald's already high rating as a singer and looker, and a good bet to regain

much of the ground lost by Chevalier in the last couple of years.

The New York Times

The new Ernst Lubitsch confection, a witty and incandescent rendition of *The Merry Widow*, had its first public hearing on this earth last night, where it was presented amid the tumult and the shouting which befit important cinema openings and perhaps the coronation of emperors. The overhead arc lamps threw a weird blue mist which was visible up and down Broadway. According to Major Bowes, whose first-hand description from the lobby came thundering to the crowds outside through a loud-speaker, enough stars were present to outfit a new universe. Mounted policemen clattered up on the sidewalk and gallantly beat back the surging proletariat. Miss MacDonald announced that her heart was full of gratitude. When Franz Lehar's name was flashed on the screen, everybody applauded, and necks were craned in an effort to discover if Mr. Lehar was in the house. Then, or a bit later, the show went on. . . . There was an inconsiderate rumor not long ago that Mr. Chevalier was diminishing in luster. Let that be spiked at once. He had never been better in voice or charm.

Naughty Marietta

A Metro-Goldwyn-Mayer Picture   1935

Produced by Hunt Stromberg. Directed by W. S. Van Dyke. Assistant director, Eddie Woehler. Screenplay by John Lee Mahin, Frances Goodrich, and Albert Hackett; based on the book by Rida Johnson Young. Photography by William Daniels. Musical adaptation, Herbert Stothart. Recording director, Douglas Shearer. Art director, Cedric Gibbons. Costumes by Adrian. Film editor, Blanche Sewell.   80 minutes.

Songs   "Chansonette," "Antoinette And Anatole," "Prayer," "Tramp, Tramp, Tramp Along the Highway," "Owl and the Pole-cat," " 'Neath the Southern Moon," "Italian Street Song," "Dance of the Marionettes," "Ship Ahoy," "I'm Falling In Love with Someone," and "Ah, Sweet Mystery of Life." Music by Victor Herbert. Lyrics by Rida Johnson Young. Additional lyrics by Gus Kahn.

CAST

Marietta-Marie de la Bonafain, JEANETTE MacDONALD; *Captain Richard Warrington,* NELSON EDDY; *Governor d'Annard,* FRANK MORGAN; *Madame d'Annard,* ELSA LANCHESTER; *Prince de la Bonafain,* Douglass Dumbrille; *Herr Schuman,* Joseph Cawthorn; *Julie,* Cecelia Parker; *Don Carlos,* Walter Kingsford; *Frau Schuman,* Greta Meyer; *Rudolpho,* Akim Tamiroff; *Abe,* Harold Huber; *Zeke,* Edward Brophy; *Felice,* Cora Sue Collins; *Casquette Girls,* Marjorie Main, Mary Doran, Jean Chatburn, Pat Farley, Jane Barnes, Jane Mercer, Linda Parker, and Kay English.

SYNOPSIS

The lovely and charming Princess Marie de la Bonafain, is to be married against her will to the odious Don Carlos de Braganza, a Spanish Grandee. Marie is an orphan and lives with her uncle, the Prince de la Bonafain. He is most desirous of having her wed Don Carlos as it is to be a diplomatic marriage sanctioned by His Majesty, Louis XV of France. Her maid, Marietta, comes to bid her farewell for she is leaving for Louisiana with the boat load of casquette girls. Marie offers to give her money that will enable her to marry her poor sweetheart who must remain in France, if she would let her take her place. Marie boards the ship as Marietta. As they near the new land, the ship is seized by a band of pirates. The girls are taken ashore by the brigands. A band of Yankee Scouts, under the leadership of handsome young Captain Warrington, rescue the girls. Marie finds herself attached to Warrington, but he curtly informs her that he has not the slightest intention of getting married, as he enjoys his life as a soldier. The girls are escorted to New Orleans where they are expected to choose husbands from the colonists. Marie doesn't want to marry any of them, so she tells the Governor that she is an immoral girl. He has her taken away from the other girls, and she gets a job in a marionette show. Warrington finds that he loves her and they are on the point of confessing mutual love when Marie is apprehended by representatives of the governor. The prince and Don Carlos arrive to take her back to France. That night a ball is given in her honor at the palace. Her uncle informs her that unless she agrees to sail for France, harm will come to Warrington. She agrees to go with her uncle. Warrington comes to the ball and she lets him think that she isn't leaving for several days. The guests beg her to sing, and in order to let Warrington know of her love for him she sings. He joins her in song. He tells her to elope with him that they will go to the wilderness where the French government can never reach her. She agrees and together they leave the palace surrounded by Warrington's faithful soldiers.

COMMENTS

This was the first MacDonald-Eddy musical film. For his first starring role, Nelson did a nice job of acting. Dr. Edouard Lippe, Nelson's vocal coach, had a bit part. Also featured were Marjorie Main, who had a bit part as a Casquette Girl, and Douglas Dumbrille, the great character actor who subsequently appeared in a few more of Jeanette's films. The comedy of Frank Morgan and Elsa

With Cecilia Parker

With Akim Tamiroff

With Joseph Cawthorn and Greta Meyer

With Frank Morgan

With Elsa Lanchester and Frank Morgan

Lanchester added much to the film. The lilting music and the superb singing of the Victor Herbert score by the stars conquered film audiences around the world.

Photoplay

A spectacle set to music—with thrills, romance and gorgeous melody in old Louisiana of Colonial days. Jeanette MacDonald and Nelson Eddy sing superbly Victor Herbert's lovely music. It's gorgeous to watch, beautiful to listen to.

Screenland

You'll thrill to this. The most distinguished singing picture of the new season, *Naughty Marietta*, has a vigor and vitality too often missing in our musical movies. Reason: First, W.S. Van Dyke's forthright direction; Second, Nelson Eddy's arresting voice and presence; Third, the color of the locale, picturesque Louisiana in the 18th Century. Of course, to me, it's Nelson Eddy's picture. Jeanette

MacDonald is charming, both vocally and optically; she endows her role of the runaway princess with gaiety and sparkle; but she is, after all, *Merry Widow* MacDonald—again, while Mr. Eddy is very new, very handsome—and different. You've never seen a movie hero like him before. He has a really splendid voice, but he appeals first of all as a manly figure, romantic but believable. As a dashing soldier of the Southland he rescues the fair princess-in-disguise from the pirates—it's that sort of a swashbuckling story—falls in love with her without learning her identity, pursues her, protects her, and finally—"Ah Sweet Mystery of Life." Victor Herbert's music lives again, beautifully sung. Don't miss it.

With James Stewart

Rose Marie
A Metro-Goldwyn-Mayer Picture   1936

Produced by Hunt Stromberg. Directed by W.S. Van Dyke. Screenplay by Frances Goodrich, Albert Hackett, and Alice Duer Miller; based on the stage production by Arthur Hammerstein; from the play by Otto Harbach and Oscar Hammerstein, II. Photography by William Daniels. Music composed by Rudolf Friml and Herbert Stothart. Musical direction by Herbert Stothart. Operatic episodes staged by William Von Wymetal. Totem Pole dance staged by Chester Hale. Recording director, Douglas Shearer. Art director, Cedric Gibbons. Associate art directors, Edwin B. Willis and Joseph Wright. Film editor, Blanche Sewell.   110 minutes.

Songs "Rose Marie," "Song of the Mounties," "Indian Love Call," "Totem Tom-Tom," music and lyrics by Rudolf Friml, Oscar Hammerstein, II, and Otto Harbach; "Romeo And Juliet" aria by Gounod; "Pardon Me Madame," music and lyrics by Gus Kahn and Herbert Stothart; "Dinah," music and lyrics by Sam Lewis, Joe Young, and Harry Akst; "Some of These Days," music and lyrics by Shelton Brooks; "Just for You," music and lyrics by Rudolf Friml, Herbert Stothart, and Gus Kahn; "Tosca," aria by Puccini.

CAST

Marie de Flor, JEANETTE MacDONALD: *Sergeant Bruce,* NELSON EDDY; *Meyerson,* Reginald Owen; *Anna,* Una O'Connor; *Boniface,* George Regas; *John Flower,* James Stewart; *Romeo,* Allan Jones; *Bella,* Gilda Gray; *Cafe Manager,* Robert Greig; *Storekeeper,* Lucien Littlefield; *Premier,* Alan Mowbray; *Teddy,* David Niven; *Mr. Daniels,* Herman Bing; *Mr. Gordon,* Halliwell Hobbes; *Emil,* Paul Porcasi; *Commandant,* Russell Hicks; *Dancers,* David Robel and Rinaldo Alacorn.

SYNOPSIS

Marie de Flor, a glamorous opera star, is on a successful tour of Canada. While in Montreal, she makes a conquest of the premier of Canada for her own purpose. She hopes to get the premier to pardon her younger brother, John Flower, imprisoned for participating in a holdup.

During a party for the Canadian officials Boniface, a half-breed, calls at her apartment and tells her that her brother Jack has escaped and killed a "mountie," that he is hiding in a shack where Boniface's mother lives in the north woods. Marie decides to accompany him and borrows her maid's shabby little valise and coat, and starts out with Boniface. On arriving at the last outpost, Marie prepares to buy suitable clothing for the remaining part of the trip. Boniface steals her purse, and the shopkeeper advises her to tell the Mounted Police about it. She doesn't want to do this. Instead, she tries to earn money by singing in a dance hall.

Sergeant Bruce, of the Mounties, who has been sent to capture Flower, recognizes the lovely diva, and when she leaves he follows her. He tells her that her suitcase is at headquarters, and she stops in to get it. He asks her what her name is, and glancing at the initial "R" on the bag, she tells him her name is Rose. He adds, "Marie de Flor." His impression is that her name is Rose Marie, but she drops the Rose part for her stage work. He offers to help her get back her purse and takes her to the place where the Indians are staging their dances. Rose Marie manages to see Boniface alone and he gives her back her money and they plan to continue the trip. Sergeant Bruce suddenly realizes that her last name is the Spanish version of Flower, and that she must be the hunted man's sister. He decides to follow

her. When Boniface sees that Bruce is following them, he bolts, leaving Rose Marie alone. Bruce takes care of her and they go on together. He finally leaves her, hoping that she will lead him to her brother. They have fallen deeply in love with each other, but he cannot shirk his duty, even though it means that he will lose her. She leads him directly to her brother, and Flower becomes his prisoner. In vain Rose Marie tries to win Bruce back to her with the Indian Love Call, which he taught her. Marie suffers a complete nervous breakdown and seems to have lost all desire to recover. Her kindly manager, knowing of her love for Bruce, sends for him. He comes to her, answering the love call as she sings it, and together their voices blend in the exquisite melody as he takes her in his arms.

COMMENTS

I never saw the earlier *Rose Marie* which was a silent film in 1928 starring Joan Crawford. This version, with the lovely voices of Jeanette and Nelson, was incomparable. The haunting music and the exquisite Totem Tom-Tom dancing add much to this beautiful romantic love story. This was the second film that starred MacDonald and Eddy and it was a box-office smash. The moment one hears the melody of "Indian Love Call" one immediately associates it as their song. Three stars emerged from this film: James Stewart, David Niven, and Allan Jones. Who could ever imagine that Allan Jones playing a bit role would next be leading man to Jeanette in *The Firefly.* My two favorite character people, Reginald Owen and Una O'Connor, were always a delight. The 1954 version of *Rose Marie* was a disappointment.

Variety

Hunt Stromberg's production hasn't spared the horses and W. S. Van Dyke's direction has blended all the virile opponents with a generous measure of basic romance to please every type of customer. He's even injected touches of humor . . . Jeanette & Nelson are in fine voice, but histrionically and cinematographically it's Miss MacDonald's edge. It's not only the best photographic job for the star, William Daniels clicked a mean lens on this chore, but her dramatic opportunities are most effective . . . *Rose Marie* is a box-office honey.

With Una O'Connor

San Francisco

A Metro-Goldwyn-Mayer Picture   1936

Produced by John Emerson and Bernard H. Hyman. Directed by W. S. Van Dyke. Assistant director, Joseph Newman. Screenplay by Anita Loos; based on the story by Robert Hopkins. Photography by Oliver T. Marsh. Musical director, Herbert Stothart. Musical score, Edward Ward. Operatic sequences staged by William Von Wymetal. Dances staged by Val Raset. Recording director, Douglas Shearer. Art director, Cedric Gibbons. Assistant art directors, Edwin B. Willis, Arnold Gillespie, and Harry McAfee. Costumes by Adrian. Montage sequences, John Hoffman. Film editor, Tom Held.   115 minutes.

Songs "San Francisco" and "The One Love," music and lyrics by Gus Kahn, Bronislau Kaper, and Walter Jurmann; "Would You," music and lyrics by Nacio Herb Brown and Arthur Freed.

CAST
Blackie Norton, CLARK GABLE; *Mary Blake,* JEANETTE MacDONALD; *Father Mullin,* SPENCER TRACY; *Jack Burley,* Jack Holt; *Mrs. Burley,* Jessie Ralph; *Mat,* Ted Healy; *Trixie,* Shirley Ross; *Della Bailey,* Margaret Irving; *Babe,* Harold Huber; *Professor,* Al Shean; *Signor Baldini,* William Ricciardi; *Chick,* Kenneth Harlan; *Alaska,* Roger Imhof; *Tony,* Charles Judels; *Red Kelly,* Russell Simpson; *Freddie Duane,* Bert Roach; *Hazeltine,* Warren Hymer; *Sheriff,* Edgar Kennedy.

With Spencer Tracy

With Clark Gable and Ted Healy

SYNOPSIS

Mary Blake comes to San Francisco, ambitious for an operatic career, but circumstances force her to accept an entertainer's position in Blackie Norton's Barbary Coast Cafe. A wealthy Nob Hill aristocrat, Jack Burley, hears her singing and offers to help her develop her career. Blackie and Burley, now rivals, determine to destroy each other. Mary's love will be the victor's reward. Then Mary discovers that Burley's intentions are not honorable. Grateful to Blackie for his help, but afraid of his intentions, she finds confidence in the council of Father Mullin, an old friend of Blackie's. Mary enters a contest and wins the first prize, which she offers to Blackie to help him. Because of a stubborn pride he rejects the prize money and Mary. A horrendous earthquake destroys the city. Blackie, realizing his love for Mary, searches for her and finds her, with Father Mullin, ministering to the injured and the dying. Blackie is grateful that Mary's life has been spared.

COMMENTS

The presently released versions of some of the MacDonald-Eddy films are now shorter than at the time of original release. This is true of all Jeanette's films. A complete and uncut final print of *San Francisco* has never been shown on television. Usually deleted is Gable's encounter with the Chinese Cook, his romance with Shirley Ross, and a carriage ride involving Jeanette and Jack Holt. Sometimes cuts are even more extensive, but these scenes are generally the ones always missing. It is believed that James Basevi, a special effects man, did the major work in engineering the earthquake scene for director W. S. Van Dyke. Gable was a very good leading man for Jeanette. The ladies in the audiences adored his virile charm. The reproduction of the earthquake of San Francisco on April 18, 1906, was realistic. Startling scenes of the sidewalks splitting and the buildings falling to the ground offered a great climax.

New York Sun

With those earthquake scenes, with Miss MacDonald's golden voice and beauty, with the dimpled Mr. Gable in a he-man role, and with Mr. Tracy quietly humorous, quietly powerful as the understanding priest, *San Francisco* does not have to worry much about length or anything else.

With Clark Gable, Jack Holt and Spencer Tracy

New York Herald Tribune, Howard Barnes:

It is a cunningly screened pattern of cinematic hokum. While the narrative is not to be recommended for its dramatic or emotional integrity, W. S. Van Dyke has shot the works in his direction and the performers have given the material the over-emphasis necessary to make it a showy entertainment. Mr. Gable, as Blackie, is the most successful member of the company . . . Spencer Tracy is not so fortunate in the part of the holy father, but the role is not one that lends itself to the actor's particular talents. . . . As for Jeanette MacDonald, she is almost entirely nonplused by proceedings. When she is chanting ragtime ditties in a Barbary Coast cabaret she is engaging and believable, but there is not much to be said for her rendition of operatic fragments when she has been taken up by the dudes, and she scarcely ever achieves any power in her straight acting.

Maytime

A Metro-Goldwyn-Mayer Picture   1937

Produced by Hunt Stromberg. Directed by Robert Z. Leonard. Screenplay by Noel Langley; based on the musical play by Rida Johnson Young and Sigmund Romberg. Photography by Oliver T. Marsh. Musical direction, Herbert Stothart. Adaptation of French Libretto by Gilles Guilbert. Vocal arrangements by Leo Arnaud. Opera sequences staged by William Von Wymetal. Recording director, Douglas Shearer. Art direction, Cedric Gibbons. Assisted by Fredric Hope and Edwin B. Willis. Gowns by Adrian. Film editor, Conrad A. Nervig.   131 minutes.

Songs "Will You Remember" and "Maytime Finale," music and lyrics by Rida Johnson Young and Sigmund Romberg; "Virginia Ham and Eggs" and "Vive L'Opera," music and lyrics by Herbert Stothart, Bob Wright, and Chet Forrest; "Student Drinking Song," music and lyrics by Herbert Stothart; "Carry Me Back to Old Virginny," music and lyrics by James A. Bland; "Czaritza," based on Tchaikovsky's Fifty Symphony, libretto by Bob Wright and Chet Forrest; "Reverie," based on Sigmund Romberg airs; "Jump Jim Crow," "Road to Paradise," and "Dancing Will Keep You Young," music and lyrics by Rida Johnson Young, Cyrus Wood, and Sigmund Romberg; "Page's Aria from *Les Huguenots* by Meyerbeer; "Les Filles de Cadiz," by Delibes; "Street Singer," music and lyrics by Chet Forrest, Bob Wright, and Herbert Stothart.

CAST

Marcia Mornay/Marcia Morrison, JEANETTE Mac-DONALD; *Paul Allison,* NELSON EDDY; *Nicolai Nazaroff,* JOHN BARRYMORE; *Archipenco,* Herman Bing; *Kip,* Tom Brown; *Barbara Roberts,* Lynne Carver; *Ellen,* Rafaela Ottiano; *Cabby,* Charles Judels; *Trentini,* Paul Porcasi; *Fanchon,* Sig Rumann; *Rudyard,* Walter Kingsford; *Secretary,* Edgar Norton; *Louis Napoleon,* Guy Bates Post; *Mme. Fanchon,* Anna Demetrio; *Orchestra Conductor,* Frank Puglia; *Maypole Dancer,* Joan Le Sueur; *Mr. Bulliet,* Russell Hicks; *Opera Directors,* Harry Davenport, Harry Hayden, Howard Hickman and Robert C. Fischer; *Drunk,* Billy Gilbert; *Student In Bar,* Leonid Kinsky and the Don Cossack Chorus.

With John Barrymore and Ivan Lebedeff

131

With Walter Kingsford, Herman Bing and John Barrymore

SYNOPSIS

In the New England village where she has lived for so long no one would have known anything about elderly Marcia Morrison were it not that her young neighbor, Barbara Roberts, contemplates deserting Kip, her village sweetheart, for a career as a singer in New York. After a quarrel with Kip, Barbara appeals to Miss Morrison asking if she isn't right to want a chance to be another Jenny Lind, Tettrazzini, or Marcia Mornay? She is sure Miss Morrison will understand her plight. Miss Morrison does indeed understand, for she was diva Marcia Mornay before retirement many years before. On a night in Paris when she sang for Emperor Louis Napoleon, the great composer Trentini had agreed to immortalize her by writing an opera for her, and the celebrated impresario Nicolai Nazaroff had asked her to marry him. Marcia did not love Nazaroff but was unable to refuse his offer because marriage was often the price of a spectacular career. Remembering other singers he trained and other demands he made, the arrangement did not seem unreasonable.

Unable to sleep after the excitement of her concert, Marcia took a carriage to the Left Bank where outside a cafe she heard students raising their voices in rollicking song. Marcia slipped into the cafe to listen to the magnificent voice of the student leader, Paul Allison. Learning Marcia was also an American, he exerted all his charms to make her promise to lunch with him on the following day. Against her better judgment she accepted the invitation. Paul was not content until she spent May Day at the St. Cloud Fair with him. By evening, Marcia and Paul were in love and unable to do anything about it. Marcia had given her promise to enter into a loveless marriage with Nazaroff and could not break it. The lovers parted and the ensuing years were crowded with triumphs for Marcia. When she arrived in New York for a brilliant American operatic debut, she found that Paul was to sing the baritone lead. The love that she had tried to deny could no longer be ignored, and after their overwhelming success, she knew that she could never again part from Paul. Engrossed in each other, they did not see a fiercely jealous Nazaroff with a pistol in his hand. He fired and Paul crumpled to the ground. In recalling all this, Marcia Mornay convinces Barbara that between love and a career there can be no choice if love is sincere.

COMMENTS

Maytime was the third co-starring film for Jeanette and

With John Barrymore

133

Nelson. Critically it is the most acclaimed of all eight films that the team did. *Maytime* was the personal favorite of Jeanette. It afforded the stars more dramatic range than in any of their other film roles. It offered them more duets to sing and was surely one of the most beautifully photographed motion pictures of the era. In 1936 Irving Thalberg, then head of MGM decided to film *Maytime* with Jeanette and Nelson. He was to personally handle the film, which marked the first time he had worked with the team, although he had worked with Jeanette on Lubitsch's version of *The Merry Widow.* The film's story was based partially on the twenties operetta, though some new material had been added. Paul Lukas was originally cast in the role of Nazaroff but was replaced by John Barrymore. Sigmund Romberg was brought to MGM to compose a score for the film. In addition to the original songs, Romberg wrote a new duet "Farewell To Dreams." This production was closed briefly because of Thalberg's untimely death. After Thalberg's funeral *Maytime* was assigned to producer Hunt Stromberg and director Robert Z. Leonard. Everything that had been done on the film up to that time was scrapped. Not knowing what Thalberg really wanted in the completed film they started all over again. The result was a far more lavish film than originally planned.

New York Times, Frank Nugent

Maytime is the most entrancing operetta the screen has given us. It establishes Jeanette MacDonald as the possessor of the cinema's loveliest voice—this with all deference to the probably superior off-screen voices of Lily Pons, Grace Moore, and Gladys Swarthout—and it affirms Nelson Eddy's pre-eminence among the baritones of filmdom. The screen can do no wrong when these two are singing, when, in addition, it places a splendid production behind them, the result approaches perfection. *Maytime* does just that.

Photoplay

With a scent of peach blossoms for mood and a superbly romantic score for background, Jeanette MacDonald and Nelson Eddy return again in this traditionally beautiful story of love, found and lost. It is gay and charming and heartstirring. It is a nostalgic thing set to music. Aside from Sigmund Romberg's "Sweethearts," Jeanette and Nelson sing a symposium of songs, including "Santa Lucia," a portion of "Les Huguenots," etc.

The opera Czaritza sequence. Jeanette as Czaritza, Mariska Aldrich as the maid/singer and a member of the Don Cossack Chorus as the priest.

The Firefly

A Metro-Goldwyn-Mayer Picture   1937

With Allan Jones

With Allan Jones

Produced by Hunt Stromberg. Directed by Robert Z. Leonard. Screenplay by Frances Goodrich and Albert Hackett; based on the book by Otto Harbach. Adaptation by Ogden Nash. Musical direction, Herbert Stothart. Dances by Albertina Rasch. Recording director, Douglas Shearer. Art director, Cedric Gibbons. Assistant art directors, Edwin B. Willis and Paul Groesse. Gowns by Adrian. Technical advisor, George Richelavie. Montage effects by Slavko Vorkapich. Film editor, Robert J. Kern. Filmed in Sepia.   140 minutes.

Songs "Love Is Like A Firefly," "He Who Loves and Runs Away," "When a Maid Comes Knocking at Your Heart," "A Woman's Kiss," "When the Wine is Full of Fire," "Sympathy," and "Giannina Mia," music and lyrics by Rudolf Friml and Otto Harbach; "The Donkey Serenade," music and lyrics by Rudolf Friml, Bob Wright, and Chet Forrest.

CAST

Nina Azara, JEANETTE MacDONALD: *Don Diego Manrique de Lara-Captain Francois de Coucourt,* ALLAN JONES; *Colonel de Rougemont,* Warren William; *Innkeeper,* Billy Gilbert; *Marquis de Melito,* Douglass Dumbrille; *Etienne,* Leonard Penn; *King Ferdinand,* Tom Rutherford; *Lola,* Belle Mitchell; *Secret Service Chief,* George Zucco; *Duval,* Corbett Morris; *Duke of Wellington,* Matthew Boulton; *Juan,* Robert Spindola; *Pablo,* Frank Puglia; *Spanish Patriot,* Jason Robards, Sr.; *French Soldier,* Alan Curtis; *French Lieutenant,* Ralph Byrd; *French Soldier Admirer,* Dennis O'Keefe; *Spanish General,* Pedro de Cordoba; *Captain Pierlot,* Theodore Von Eltz.

SYNOPSIS

Madrid, 1808. In one of the principal cafes, Nina Azara dances and sings. Don Diego Manrique de Lara, wealthy young Spaniard with whom Nina deliberately flirts in order to rid herself of her former admirer, Etienne, a French officer. Nina in reality is a Spanish spy hired by the Marquis de Melito, adviser to King Ferdinand, to discover Napoleon's plan of invasion.

In Bayonne, Nina loses no time in ingratiating herself with Colonel de Rougemont, one of Napoleon's staff officers. Nina appeals to Don Diego for help only to learn that he is in reality a French spy whose duty is to trail her. King Ferdinand is forced to abdicate and Joseph Bonaparte is declared king. Nina upbraids herself for having failed.

Five years of war elapse, the English having come to help the Spanish. Nina, behind the French lines again, meets de Rougemont, now a General, who wants to resume their affair. But once again, through Don Diego, alias Captain Francois Andre, Nina is proved to be a spy carrying a map of the French lines. She is sentenced to execution. Don Diego comes to see her, heartbroken, telling her that duty again forced him to betray her. It had been Nina's plan that she should be caught with the map of the French positions in order to lure them into changing them. Otherwise, they would have been impregnable. Don Diego, rushing to join his regiment, drops wounded almost at the cell door. The English and Spanish are triumphant and Napoleon is driven from Spain. Nina discovers Don Diego in a field hospital. The war over, there is no barrier left between them. They ride away together on the same mountain road where once he had followed her in her coach.

COMMENTS

When Jeanette was called back to the studio for several retakes just three days before her wedding, she agreed to do this rather than have to postpone her honeymoon in Hawaii. Based on a 1911 operetta, this was the only film version made of the Friml operetta, which starred Emma Trentini and Henry Vogel on Broadway. The film was shot almost entirely at the MGM Studios except for the scenes depicting the Pyrenees mountains. These were shot on location at Lone Pine at the foot of the Sierras. Two new songs were added to the screen version. Rudolf Friml borrowed his "He Who Loves and Runs Away" from another score and made it a big production number for Jeanette. For Allan Jones' solo he rewrote an old song that had not been popular, neither as a lullaby, "In Love," nor as a foxtrot titled "Chanson." He changed the tempo a third time and called it "The Donkey Serenade" for the film version! In the number, "When a Maid Comes Knocking at Your Heart," Jeanette does her own piano playing, which she did in all her films, since she was an accomplished musician as well as a singer.

With Theodore Von Eltz

With Warren William

With Ralph Byrd

Journal American

Large, lavish spectacle, rare singing, one of the studios most pretentious musicals.

Daily Variety

Produced with magnificence, alive with the stirring lilt of music and projecting a superlative love story which rises to passionate dramatic heights. A delight to any audience. Scenes are played with genuine emotion and appeal, the singing catches the heart. Jeanette MacDonald is superb. Enchantress as well as lover, she displays versatility in beguiling seductions, in passionate dancing, in finely shaded moods of dread, concern and surrender. The production is lavish and elegant, with a wealth of entertainment for the widest possible appeal.

Rosalie

A Metro-Goldwyn-Mayer Picture   1937

Produced by William Anthony McGuire. Directed by W. S. Van Dyke. Assistant director, William Scully. Screenplay by William Anthony McGuire; based on the play by William Anthony McGuire and Guy Bolton, as produced on the stage by Florenz Ziegfeld. Photography by Oliver T. Marsh. Montage effects by Slavko Vorkapich. Musical direction, Herbert Stothart. Musical presentation, Merrill Pye. Musical conductor, Georgie Stoll. Musical arrangements by Roger Edens. Vocal and orchestral arrangements by Leo Arnaud, Murray Cutter, Leon Rabb, and Paul Marquardt. Opening Romanza sequence, incidental music by Cole Porter. "The Polovetzian Dances," music by Alexander Borodin. "M'Apari" an aria from the opera, *Martha*, Music by Von Flotow. "Stars And Stripes Forever," music by John Phillip Sousa. "Oh, Promise Me," music by Reginald De Koven, lyrics by Clement Scott. "The Caissons Go Rolling Along," music and lyrics by Edmund L. Gruber. "Anchors Aweigh," music by Charles A. Zimmerman, lyrics by Alfred A. Miles and Royal Lovell. Dances and Ensembles created and staged by Albertina Rasch, assisted by Dave Gould. Recording director, Douglas Shearer. Art Director, Cedric Gibbons. Assisted by Joseph Wright and Edwin B. Willis. Costumes by Dolly Tree. Film editor, Blanche Sewell.   122 minutes.

Songs   "Rosalie," "Who Knows," "In the Still of the Night," "Why Should I Care," "I've A Strange New Rhythm in My Heart," "Close," "National Anthem," "It's All Over But the Shouting," "I Know It's Not Meant for Me," "Spring Love Is in the Air," "To Love or Not to Love," and "On, Brave Old Army Team." Music and lyrics by Cole Porter.

With Ray Bolger

CAST

Dick Thorpe, NELSON EDDY; *Rosalie,* ELEANOR POWELL; *Brenda,* ILONA MASSEY; *Bill Delroy,* Ray Bolger; *King Frederic,* Frank Morgan; *Queen,* Edna May Oliver; *First Officer (Oloff)* Billy Gilbert; *Chancellor,* Reginald Owen; *General Maroff,* George Zucco; *Mary Callahan,* Virginia Grey; *Prince Paul,* Tom Rutherford; *Miss Baker,* Janet Beecher; *Captain Banner,* Clay Clement; *Mr. Callahan,* Oscar O'Shea; *Army's Coach,* William Demarest; *Herman Schmidt,* Al Shean; *Lady In Waiting,* Katherine Aldridge.

With Ilona Massey

With Eleanor Powell

SYNOPSIS

At an Army-Navy football game, Cadet Dick Thorpe, a West Pointer, makes the winning play, much to the delight of Rosalie, a princess of Romanza, who is a student incognito at Vassar. Rosalie must return to Romanza to wed a prince in a loveless marriage and Dick Thorpe flies across the Atlantic to keep his date with her at a native festival. Although Rosalie in the beginning believes him to be very conceited, she soon falls in love with him and he with her. The royal family is forced to flee Romanza. They take refuge in the U.S. where Rosalie and Dick are reunited.

COMMENTS

MGM attempted a production of *Rosalie* with Marion Davies in the title role but abandoned it and no footage was retained for the 1937 film. This film marked Ilona Massey's screen debut. Ray Bolger was taken out of *Rose Marie* and was signed for a supporting role in *Rosalie*.

MGM gave Nelson two leading ladies, Eleanor Powell and Miss Massey, though Miss Powell won him in the end.

Photoplay

Metro spent about $2,000,000 on this and it ought to be something pretty special. That it turns out to be just a good show in fancy dress may be the result of too many expectations, or it may be that mixing a West Point football story with a mythical kingdom romance was not such a great idea. Still, for your money you get the greatest set ever constructed anywhere, a generous helping of Nelson Eddy singing good old Cole Porter tunes, plenty of Eleanor Powell's dancing, lots of Frank Morgan's funny hesitating speech, and a lot of other things too numerous to list here. Ilona Massey, attractive newcomer, sings beautifully. Ray Bolger is Eddy's pal. "Rosalie" and "In The Still of the Night" are hummable tunes.

The Girl of the Golden West

A Metro-Goldwyn-Mayer Picture   1938

With Buddy Ebsen

144

With Walter Pidgeon

Produced by William Anthony McGuire. Directed by Robert Z. Leonard. Screenplay by Isabel Dawn and Boyce DeGaw; based on the play by David Belasco. Photography by Oliver T. Marsh. Musical direction, Herbert Stothart. Orchestral and vocal arrangements, Leonid Raab, Leo Arnaud, Murray Cutter, and Paul Marquardt. Musical presentation, Merrill Pye. Dances and ensembles created and staged by Albertina Rasch. Recording director, Douglas Shearer. Art Director, Cedric Gibbons. Assistant art directors, Edwin B. Willis and Eddie Imazu. Montage effects, Slavko Vorkapich. Gowns by Adrian. Film editor, W. Donn Hayes. Filmed in Sepia.   120 minutes.

Songs "Soldiers of Fortune," "Shadows on the Moon," "Gentle Wind in the Trees," "Senorita," "Mariache," "Sun Up To Sun Down," "The West Ain't Wild Any Mo," and "Who Are We to Say," music by Sigmund Romberg, lyrics by Gus Kahn. "Liebestraum" (Dream of Love) by Franz Liszt. "Ave Maria" by Gounod-Bach).

With Leo Carrillo

CAST

Mary Robbins, JEANETTE MacDONALD; *Ramerez-Lieutenant Johnson,* NELSON EDDY; *Jack Rance,* Walter Pidgeon; *Mosquito,* Leo Carrillo; *Alabama,* Buddy Ebsen; *Pedro,* Leonard Penn; *Nina Martinez,* Priscilla Lawson; *Sonora Slim,* Bob Murphy; *Trinidad Joe,* Olin Howland; *Minstrel Joe,* Cliff Edwards; *Nick,* Billy Bevan; *The Professor* Brandon Tynan; *Father Sienna,* H.B. Warner; *Governor,* Monty Woolley; *Uncle Davey,* Charley Grapewin; *The General,* Noah Beery, Sr.; *Pioneer,* Russell Simpson; *Mary (as a girl),* Jeanne Ellis; *Gringo,* Bill Cody, Jr.

SYNOPSIS

Mary Robbins is the owner of the Polka Saloon in Cloudy Mountain. It is time for her to visit Father Sienna in Monterey, and also do some shopping for the Polka. On the mountain road, Ramerez and his bandits rob the stage coach, but Mary outwits him by hiding her gold in a papoose basket. He permits the coach to continue, but he is stricken by Mary's beauty. Accompanied by Mosquito, he follows her to Monterey. At the parish church, the padre tells Mary of mysterious contributions he has been receiving. Ramerez overhears the governor inviting Mary to a

ball and fiesta. On the following night, while preparing for the ball, Mary is told that Lieutenant Johnson awaits her. It is Ramerez, although she does not recognize him in a stolen uniform. He becomes a bit too amorous. She slaps him, jumps into the carriage and drives to the ball without the lieutenant. Rance tells Mary of his trap to catch Ramerez, forbidding any gold to be sent from Cloudy and keeping it at the Polka. Boldly, Ramerez enters the Polka Saloon. Rance eyes him suspiciously, but Mary vouches for the stranger.

Mary invites him to supper in her cabin the next night. That night, while he is in Mary's cabin, Ramerez hides as Rance and some deputies enter. Rance tells Mary about Nina, Ramerez's native sweetheart, and Mary's love for Ramerez turns to hatred. She hears two shots outside, then a thump at the door. Opening it, she finds Ramerez shot through the shoulder. She hides him in the loft and Rance comes back. She denies that she is hiding Ramerez but a drop of blood falls from the loft onto Rance's hand. Ramerez comes down, and Mary pleads for his life.

Rance agrees to cut cards with Mary for Ramerez's life. Mary wins. He discovers that Mary has won by cheating. Again Mary pleads and Rance agrees to give Ramerez another chance. He turns Ramerez loose and, as her part of the bargain, Mary consents to marry him. At the chapel in Monterey, Mary hears a familiar voice singing outside. It is Ramerez. When Rance again sees them together, he is determined to kill Ramerez, but he decides to give him an even break. He hands a gun to Ramerez and tells him to walk around the chapel. Rance will walk in the opposite direction. When they meet, they will fire. Mary collapses in the padre's arms. When she looks up again, Ramerez is standing in front of her. Rance had failed to circle the church and vanished. She drops her head on Ramerez's shoulder, weeping with joy.

COMMENTS

This was Jeanette and Nelson's fourth film together. *The Girl of the Golden West* had been produced on the New York stage, November 14, 1905, with Blanche Bates and Robert Hilliard in the lead roles. In 1914, the Jesse L. Lasky Company filmed a silent version that was directed and produced by Cecil B. DeMille with Mabel Van Buren,

House Peters, and Theodore Roberts starred. In 1923, First National produced a second silent version with Edwin Carewe directing and featuring Sylvia Breamer, J. Warren Kerrigan and Russell Simpson. In 1930 First National Pictures screened a talking picture directed by John Francis Dillion in which Ann Harding, James Rennie, and Harry Bannister starred.

When Jeanette and Nelson sing the Sigmund Romberg music, which was written for the new film version of *The Girl of the Golden West*, they both give a lift to the film. Metro-Goldwyn-Mayer chose to eliminate the score of "La Faniculla del West" by Giacomo Puccini, who used it as the basis of his opera in 1919. They signed Sigmund Romberg to write the music. Since the Puccini arias couldn't be used they decided to use "Liebestraum" and "Ave Maria" for Jeanette to sing and which she sang with feeling. The film is in the soft sepia-tone which is very suitable for outdoor filming. I enjoyed everyone's performance and H.B. Warner gave a moving performance, as always, in the role of a sympathetic priest.

Liberty Magazine—Ruth Waterbury

For Jeanette MacDonald-Nelson Eddy enthusiasts we give this three stars. For others, we warn you that the production has about as much zip as a turtle who's had a busy day. It's two hours are definitely pleasant and sentimental but they do drag. The usual MacDonald-Eddy ingredients (a passionate lonely love song for Jeanette, followed by a passionate lonely love song for Nelson, followed sometime later by a passionate love duet for the two of them) have been stirred here into a story as dated and as pretty as Grandma's wedding gown. Jeanette is "the girl." That is all the rough cowboys down at the saloon ever call her; but, gosh, how they respect her. And Nelson is the mysterious stranger, actually the feared bandit Ramerez, a dangerous guy with a heart of pure platinum. Opposed to them is Walter Pidgeon, as Jack Rance, the sheriff, who loves the girl too. When Nelson steps in, you can see what a tidy, melodramatic little triangle is set up. All this has been staged lavishly, with the color of young California at the turn of the century nicely captured. The stars are both in excellent voice, and Miss MacDonald despite her "you all" lines, makes an appealing figure of the untutored, lovesick girl.

Sweethearts

Technicolor
A Metro-Goldwyn-Mayer Picture   1938

With Florence Rice, Terry Kilburn, Gene Lockhart, Berton Churchill, Raymond Walburn, Kathleen Lockhart and Lucile Watson.

Produced by Hunt Stromberg. Directed by W. S. Van Dyke. Screenplay by Dorothy Parker and Alan Campbell; based on the operetta with book and lyrics by Fred de Gresac, Harry B. Smith, and Robert B. Smith with music by Victor Herbert. Photography by Oliver T. Marsh and Allen Davey. Technicolor consultant, Natalie Kalmus; associate, Henri Jaffa. Montage effect by Slavko Vorkapich. Musical adaptation by Herbert Stothart. Musical presentation by Merrill Pye. Dances and ensembles by Albertina Rasch. Recording director, Douglas Shearer. Art Director, Cedric Gibbons; associate, Joseph Wright. Set decorations by Edwin B. Willis. Gowns by Adrian. Film editor, Robert J. Kern.   120 minutes.

Songs "Wooden Shoes," "For Ev'ry Lover Must Meet His Fate," "Sweethearts," "Pretty as a Picture," "The Game of Love," "Mademoiselle on Parade," "Summer Serenade," "Marching On Parade," music by Victor Her-

bert with special lyrics by Chet Forrest and Bob Wright. "Little Grey Home in the West," music by Herman Lohr, lyrics by D. Eardley-Wilmot.

CAST

Gwen Marlowe, JEANETTE MacDONALD; *Ernest Lane,* NELSON EDDY; *Felix Lehman,* Frank Morgan; *Fred,* Ray Bolger; *Kay Jordan,* Florence Rice; *Leo Kronk,* Mischa Auer; *Hannah,* Fay Holden; *Gwen's brother,* Terry Kilburn; *Una Wilson,* Betty Jaynes; *Harvey Horton,* Douglas McPhail; *Norman Trumpett,* Reginald Gardiner; *Oscar Engel,* Herman Bing; *Dink Rogers,* Allyn Joslyn; *Orlando Lane,* Raymond Walburn; *Mrs. Merrill,* Lucile Watson; *Samuel Silver,* Philip Loeb; *Aunt Amelia,* Kathleen Lockhart; *Augustus,* Gene Lockhart; *Sheridan Lane,* Berton Churchill; *Appleby,* Olin Howland; *Pianist,* Dalies Frantz.

SYNOPSIS

Gwen Marlowe and Ernest Lane are celebrating their sixth wedding anniversary as man and wife as well as being the darlings of Broadway. They've been turning a deaf ear to all Hollywood offers until they now find that they are bored with their show and its perpetual routine, of broadcasts, recordings, and publicity stunts. Tired and disillusioned, they suspend their quarrels and agree to sign a film contract. In order to keep the stars in New York, Felix Lehman, the show's producer conspires with his librettist, Leo Kronk, to have Gwen believe that Ernest is in love with their secretary Kay Jordan. The stars quarrel and agree to go their separate ways, both taking a road company on tour. Meanwhile, Leon's play is produced and it's a disaster. A review of the play in *Variety* discloses to Gwen and Ernest that Leon tricked them by reading the plot of his play to Gwen and leaving her to believe that it was based on Ernest's life. The pair return to New York to confront Felix who, with a great show of humility, says that he guesses that they've outgrown Broadway. Indignant at being considered disloyal, they decide to re-open *Sweethearts.*

COMMENTS

Sweethearts still stands as one of the most beautiful color films of the decade. This was the first Technicolor vehicle for Jeanette and Nelson. Jeanette appeared in the first scene in a blonde pigtail wig only to be able to take it off later and reveal her beautiful red hair in vivid color. Nominated for two Academy Awards, best sound recording and best score, the picture won a special award for Oliver Marsh and Allen Davey for cinematography. The stage production starred Christine MacDonald and Thomas Conkey and opened on Broadway on September 8, 1913. It was revived on Broadway again on January 21, 1947 and starred Bobby Clark.

The New York Times—Bosley Crowther

The most sumptuous Christmas package, of course, is always the one from Metro-Goldwyn-Mayer. This year it is called *Sweethearts,* is addressed to the Capitol Theatre, the same as ever, and is such a dream of ribbons, tinsel, Technicolor and sweet theatrical sentiment that it suggests a collaboration of all the leading steamer-basket architects between Fifth and Lexington Avenues. On the musical side it is also a collaborative triumph for Jeanette MacDonald and Nelson Eddy, who have never been more flatteringly recorded, or photographed, either Miss MacDonald is es-

1055-41

pecially effective in Technicolor, with all that red hair, not to mention Victor Herbert, the popular song writer. Although in the long run *Sweethearts* must be classified as a superlatively elaborate example of cinematic pastry-cookery, the MacDonald-Eddy bloc—the only one left in the metropolitan area which bursts into idolatrous applause at the mere sound of a beloved voice—must likewise be conciliated with the admission that Jeanette and Nelson have never sung or acted with more fire and abandon than they discover in the present vehicle . . . But being from Metro-Goldwyn-Mayer, *Sweethearts* is a package that you never seem to get through unpacking, even in two hours.

The National Board of Review:
   A lavish production done in Technicolor well acted with song hits.

"Pretty as a Picture"

Let Freedom Ring

Filmed in Sepia
A Metro-Goldwyn-Mayer Picture   1939

Produced by Harry Rapf. Directed by Jack Conway. Screenplay by Ben Hecht. Photography by Sidney Wagner. Musical direction by Arthur Lange. Orchestral arrangements by Leonid Raib. Recording director, Douglas Shearer. Montage effects by John Hoffman. Art director, Cedric Gibbons; associate, David Cathcart. Set decorations by Edwin B. Willis. Women's costumes by Dolly Tree. Men's costumes by Valle. Film editor, Frederick Y. Smith.   100 minutes.

Songs "Dusty Road," music by Leon Rene, lyrics by Otis Rene. "Love Serenade," music by Riccardo Drigo, lyrics by Chet Forrest and Bob Wright. "Home Sweet Home," music by Sir Henry R. Bishop, lyrics by John Howard Payne. "When Irish Eyes Are Smiling," music by Ernest R. Ball, lyrics by Chauncey Olcott and George Graff, Jr. "America," by Samuel Francis Smith. "Pat Sez He" music by Foster Carling, lyrics by Phil Ohman. "Where Else But Here," music by Sigmund Romberg, lyrics by Edward Heyman.

With Edward Arnold and Victor McLaglen

CAST

Steve Logan, NELSON EDDY; *Maggie Adams,* VIRGINIA BRUCE; *Tom Logan,* Lionel Barrymore; *Jim Wade,* Edward Arnold; *Mulligan,* Victor McLaglen; *The Mackerel,* Charles Butterworth; *Judge Bronson,* Guy Kibbee; *Rutledge,* H. B. Warner; *Underwood,* Raymond Walburn; *Ma Logan,* Sarah Padden; *Gagan,* Trevor Bardette; *Ned Wilkie,* Louis Jean Heydt; *Cockney,* Billy Bevan; *German,* Lionel Royce; *Swede,* Emory Parnell; *Tony,* Luis Alberni.

With Virginia Bruce

153

With Raymond Walburn and Charles Butterworth

With Dick Rich, Lionel Barrymore, Edward Arnold and H. B. Warner

SYNOPSIS

The farmers have been fighting the new railroad and its unscrupulous backer, Jim Wade. They see a champion in Steve Logan, who has just returned from college. An attempt is made to burn Tom Logan's home and in the melee, Steve is wounded. Since Wade has bought the town's judge, Steve pretends to see things Wade's way in the hope of routing his cutthroats and him. He's considered a Judas by all, but secretly he begins his campaign against Wade. Under the guise of "The Hornet," he kidnaps the town's publisher and his printing press and takes them to his mountain hideout. Steve then prints leaflets against Wade and has them distributed to the railroad men. An angered Wade and his henchman, Mulligan, lead a posse to find the Hornet. The farmers try to protect the Hornet from the posse, and in the battle Tom Logan is severely wounded. While Wade is trying to learn the Hornet's identity from Tom Logan, Steve reveals himself to Mulligan. After a fist fight, Mulligan agrees to join Steve against Wade. With Mulligan's aid, Wade is driven out of town and all ends well.

With Edward Arnold and Virginia Bruce

COMMENTS

Let Freedom Ring was originally titled *Song of the West.* Then it was changed to *Song of the Plains* and finally to *Let Freedom Ring.* However, it was shown under a different title overseas.

Variety:

Let Freedom Ring is momentous. It's packed with box office potentialities and audience appeal. . . . In handling the lead assignment to Nelson Eddy, Metro apparently decided to provide him with a role that calls for a square jaw and a pair of handy fists. He takes full advantage of the opportunity, displaying a vigorous characterization of the western youth who battles all comers when necessary. Battle in the cave between Eddy and McLaglen is excitingly staged. . . . Virginia Bruce makes a lovely western heroine.

Photoplay:

This is the picture in which Nelson Eddy beats up Victor McLaglen in a fist fight. That alone should be enough to make you spend your money at the box office. But there's a lot more; once again, as in "Jesse James," the railroad

plays the villain. Nelson will probably gain new fans through his portrayal of Steve Logan, who wages a winning fight for the ranchers against the suave villainy of Edward Arnold, shyster promoter, and his henchmen. After the long run of the MacDonald-Eddy musicals, you may have to get used to Nelson in this type of film, but he adapts well; and you will like the strong blend of drama, music and action. The songs with all male voices are highly effective, particularly, "Dusty Road."

With Al Shean and Lew Ayres

With Lew Ayres

Broadway Serenade

A Metro-Goldwyn-Mayer Picture   1939

Produced and directed by Robert Z. Leonard. Screenplay by Charles Lederer; from a story by Lew Lipton, John Taintor Foote, and Hans Kraly. Photography by Oliver T. Marsh. Musical direction, Herbert Stothart. Vocal and orchestrations, Leo Arnaud and Leonid Raab. Musical presentation, Merrill Pye. Dances staged by Busby Berkeley and Seymour Felix. Recording director, Douglas Shearer. Art director, Cedric Gibbons. Associate art director, Joseph Wright. Set decorations, Edwin B. Willis. Gowns by Adrian. Men's costumes by Valle. Makeup created by Jack Dawn. Montage effects, John Hoffman. Film editor, Harold Kress.   114 minutes.

Songs   "For Every Lonely Heart" and "Rhapsody," music by Herbert Stothart and Edward Ward, lyrics by Gus Kahn. "Flying High" and "One Look At You," music by Herbert Stothart and Edward Ward, lyrics by Bob Wright and Chet Forrest. "Time Changes Everything," music by Walter Donaldson, lyrics by Gus Kahn. "No Time to Argue," music by Sigmund Romberg, lyrics by Gus Kahn. "Ridin' on a Rainbow," music and lyrics by Bob Wright and Chet Forrest.

CAST

Mary Hale, JEANETTE MacDONALD; *James Seymour,* LEW AYRES; *Larry Bryant,* Ian Hunter; *Cornelius Collier, Jr.,* Frank Morgan; *Judy Tyrrell,* Rita Johnson; *Pearl,* Virginia Grey; *Joey The Jinx,* Wally Vernon; *Bill,* William Gargan; *Harriet Ingalis,* Katherine Alexander; *Herman,* Al Shean; *Mrs. Olsen,* Esther Dale; *Gene,* Franklin Pangborn; *Reynolds,* Paul Hurst; *Everett,* E. Allyn Warren; *Mr. Fellowes,* Frank Orth; *Mrs. Fellowes,* Esther Howard; *Squeaker,* Leon Belasco; *Singer,* Kenneth Stevens.

With Ian Hunter and Lew Ayres

Singing *Madame Butterfly* aria "Un Bel Di"

With Lew Ayres

SYNOPSIS

Mary Hale and her husband Jimmy Seymour lose their jobs in a cafe due to Jimmy's hot-headedness. Upon returning to their rooms, they find that Jimmy has won a scholarship to study music abroad. To obtain additional funds so that Mary can accompany him, he tries to sell one of his songs to producer Cornelius Collier. However, Mary gets to audition through the efforts of the show's "angel" Larry Bryant and joins the show just as it is about to leave for the out-of-town tryouts. Mary and the show are an immediate success. When Jimmy hears of a supposed romance between Mary and Larry, he becomes jealous, and Mary, heartbroken, obtains a divorce. Jimmy tries to destroy his manuscripts, but with the aid of his friend Herman, he decides to work hard so that he may be a success and win Mary back. Eventually, Jimmy completes a symphonic fantasy which he's certain will be a hit. He goes to break the news to Mary only to find that she's announced her coming marriage to Larry. Meanwhile, Jimmy's work is bought by Collier who intends to star Mary in the show. Larry sees that Mary still loves Jimmy and bows out. Mary and Jimmy are reunited and Mary and the show, with Jimmy's music, become a hit.

COMMENTS

Vocally and pictorially the highlight of the film was the *Madame Butterfly* aria "Un Bel Di." The sequence was staged by Seymour Felix. MGM signed Busby Berkeley to a long term contract and *Broadway Serenade* was his first film under the MGM banner. He staged the finale for the film. Berkeley and Jeanette's styles, somehow, just didn't seem to click. At the grand finale, he had her standing on a forty-foot column with the chorus standing way below her, looking up. The extras seemed in awe of Jeanette. This was not a typical reaction to Jeanette, for a great deal of the charm of other MacDonald films was her sparkle and response to everyone in the cast.

The New York Times

A sinister character named Joey the Jinx appears in the course of the Capitol's *Broadway Serenade* and threatens to put the evil eye on Frank Morgan's revue unless he gets $50 a week. Mr. Morgan has him thrown out. Poor Mr. Morgan. Poor MGM . . . Poor us . . . Joey must have been lurking around the studio with a nasty ogle when the picture was made; he must have been hiding under the Capi- tol's divans yesterday. Something went wrong with the sound equipment, then something went wrong with the projection. For awhile it was impossible to see anything, then to hear anything. But it didn't last long enough. We still know we were in the presence of the biggest bad show of the year.

Balalaika

A Metro-Goldwyn-Mayer Picture   1939

With Ilona Massey

Produced by Lawrence Weingarten. Directed by Reinhold Schunzel. Assistant director, Dolph Zimmer. Screenplay by Leon Gordon, Charles Bennett, and Jacques Deval. Contributors to screenplay construction, Vincent Lawrence and Richard Connell. Based on the play with book and lyrics by Eric Maschwitz with music by George Posford and Bernard Grun. Photography by Joseph Ruttenberg and Karl Freund. Musical adaptation and score by Herbert Stothart. Musical conductor, Dr. William Axt. Orchestrations by Murray Cutter, Paul Marquardt, and Wally Heglin. Recording director, Douglas Shearer. Art direction by Cedric Gibbons; associate, Eddie Imazu. Set directions by Edwin B. Willis. Gowns by Adrian. Russian Cossack Choir director, Anatol Frikin. Film editor, George Boemler.   102 minutes.

Songs "At The Balalaika," "Tanya," "Ride Cossack Ride," "Shadows on the Sand," and "Tale of the Tailors," music by Herbert Stothart, lyrics by Chet Forrest and Bob Wright. "Beneath the Winter's Snow," "In a Heart as Brave as Your Own," "Soldiers of the Czar," music by Sigmund Romberg, lyrics by Gus Kahn. "How Many Miles to Go," music by Herbert Stothart, lyrics by M. Glinka, "The Magic of Your Love," music by Franz Lehar, lyrics by Gus Kahn. "My Heart Is a Gypsy," music by Bronislau Kaper, lyrics by Gus Kahn.

Additional Music "Toreador Song" (Bizet's *Carmen*), "Gypsy Song" (Act II from *Carmen*) "Love Duet" (Act IV from *Carmen*), Opera sequence music based on Rimsky-Korsakov's, "Scheherezade," "The Russian National Athem," and "Silent Night."

CAST

Peter Karagin, NELSON EDDY; *Lydia Marakova*, ILONA MASSEY; *Nicki*, Charles Ruggles; *Danchenoff*, Frank Morgan; *Marakov*, Lionel Atwill; *General Karagin*, C. Aubrey Smith; *Masha*, Joyce Compton; *Sibirsky*, Walter Woolf King; *Dimitri*, Dalies Frantz; *Ramensky*, Frederick Worlock; *Leo*, Abner Biberman; *Lieut. Smirnoff*, Phillip Terry; *Batoff*, Charles Judels; *Slaski*, George Tobias; *Anton*, Paul Sutton; *Olga*, Marla Shelton; *Nina*, Kay Sutton; *Secretary to Danchenoff*, Ernest Verebes; *Proprietor*, Frank Puglia; *Mr. Morrison*, Andrew Tombes; *Mrs. Morrison*, Florence Shirley; Additional players were: Gene Ringgold, Zeffie Tilbury, George Meeker, Judith Allen, Alma Kruger, Irra Petina, and Paul Irving.

With Charles Judels

With Ilona Massey, Lionel
Atwill, Abner Biberman,
Dalies Frantz

With Ilona Massey

SYNOPSIS

Although the men in Lydia Marakova's family have all devoted themselves to the Bolshevik cause, she is attracted to Prince Karagin, who masquerades as a proletarian when he finds her singing in a popular tavern. Karagin has her pose as a music student and arranges for her debut at the Imperial Opera.

On Lydia's opening night, Karagin's father is shot by Red conspirators, among whom is Lydia's father. Lydia, furious at what she considers Karagin's betrayal of her, welcomes her banishment to Siberia with other members of her family. Karagin joins his regiment to fight the enemy. Upon his return to St. Petersburg, the revolution erupts but he manages to escape to Paris where he becomes a folk singer in a restaurant managed by former Russian nobility.

Lydia turns up there one night and she and Karagin, realizing their undying devotion to each other, are reconciled.

NOTES

In their second film together Eddy and Ilona Massey found roles that showed them both to good advantage. Eddy's singing of *Silent Night* ranks as one of his supreme camera moments as did Miss Massey's rendition of *At The Balalaika*. The supporting company was a strong one, especially Lionel Atwill, Frank Morgan, and Charles Ruggles. The two latter players were making one of their rare joint appearances since their *Queen High* triumph on Broadway in the twenties. And the beautiful Miss Massey never again showed to such lovely advantage as she did in her role of the ardent revolutionary.

Time

Balalaika is the first picture in which Ilona Massey has her first chance to star. Unfortunately, Hollywood has now got the idea that "social significance" has something to do with the amusement business. So the picture, which takes its name from a truncated Russian mandolin, the Balalaika, includes not only fatuously lovable grand dukes and musicians, but downright sinister Bolsheviks. It also includes Baritone Nelson Eddy, the Russian Cossack Choir, an excellent cast, and a lot of gorgeous clothing and sets.

The Commonweal

Nelson Eddy's singing, "Stille Nacht" in the trenches before an attack will bring forth many a tear. And so will the lavish finale when the lovers are reunited and the nobility gather in Paris to sigh over dear, dead, old Russia.

New Moon

A Metro-Goldwyn-Mayer Picture   1940

Produced and directed by Robert Z. Leonard. Screenplay by Jacques Deval and Robert Arthur; based on the operetta with music by Sigmund Romberg and book and lyrics by Oscar Hammerstein, II, Frank Mandel, and Lawrence Schwab. Photography by William Daniels. Musical direction by Herbert Stothart. Dances by Val Raset. Recording director, Douglas Shearer. Art director, Cedric Gibbons, associate, Eddie Imazu. Set decorations by Edwin B. Willis. Gowns by Adrian. Men's costumes by Gile Steele. Makeup created by Jack Dawn. Film editor, Harold F. Kress.   105 minutes.

Songs "Lover, Come Back to Me," "Wanting You," "Softly as In a Morning Sunrise," "Stout Hearted Men," "One Kiss," "Stranger In Paree," "Wedding Party," and "Marianne," music by Sigmund Romberg, lyrics by Oscar Hammerstein, II. "Bayou Trouble Tree," music by Herbert Stothart, lyrics by D. Jones. "Vespers," from *Largo* by Handel. "The Marseillaise" (French National Anthem).

CAST

Marianne de Beaumanoir, JEANETTE MacDONALD; *Charles, Duc de Villiers,* NELSON EDDY; *Valerie de Rossac,* Mary Boland; *Vicomte Ribaud,* George Zucco; *Father Michel,* H. B. Warner; *Governor of New Orleans,* Grant Mitchell; *Tambour,* Stanley Fields; *Alexander,* Richard (Dick) Purcell; *Pierre Brugnon,* John Miljan; *Guizot,* Ivan Simpson; *Pierre,* William Tannen; *Julie,* Bunty Cutler; *Monsieur Dubois,* Claude King; *Governor's Wife,* Cecil Cunningham; *Maurice,* Joe Yule; *Ship's Captain,* George Irving; *Captain de Jean,* Edwin Maxwell; *Guard on ship,* Paul Burns; *Monsieur de Piron,* Rafael Storm; *Lady,* Winifred Harris.

With Grant Mitchell and Mary Boland

SYNOPSIS

Marianne de Beaumanoir is en route from Paris to New Orleans to look over a plantation in the New World left her by an uncle. On the same ship, concealed in the hold, is a motley collection of humanity, bondsmen taken to the Southern city to be sold into slavery. Among these men is Charles, Duc de Villiers, a political enemy of the king who has escaped execution by posing as a bondsman. He has been purchased by Marianne's plantation manager as a new slave. Commenting upon his fine manners, Charles tells her that he was formerly employed by the Duc de Villiers. The romance, however, is rudely broken into when a French official arrives at the plantation and reveals the identity of her servant. Charles, who hears the conversation, loses no time in organizing the escape he has been planning for himself as well as for the other bondsmen. Seizing a ship in the harbor, the troops sail away.

Marianne, disillusioned, decides to return to Paris and talks the police captain into permitting her to sail on his boat the *New Moon,* which, he informs her, must stop at Martinique. The *New Moon* is set upon by a pirate vessel. When their vessel sinks, the pirates board the *New Moon* and take over. Marianne discovers that their leader is Charles. Together, then, this strange assorted group make their way. A fierce storm at sea, however, batters the *New Moon* and to escape with their lives the passengers and crew manage to land on an island. Not until the sails of a French ship are sighted and Charles determines to give himself up to French justice rather than endanger the lives of the colonists does Marianne really let him know of her love. When the ship finally flies the flag of truce and representatives land on the island, they bring the news that the French Revolution has triumphed and that Charles is free.

With Buster Keaton (who was replaced after start of film) and William Tannen, Nat Pendleton and unidentified player

167

With Rafael Storm

COMMENTS

New Moon first came to light on Broadway in 1928. Its initial try-out was a failure and the score and the story had to be rewritten. The original score did not contain "Lover, Come Back to Me" or "Wanting You." After much reworking the operetta opened to enthusiastic audiences and played over 500 performances. In 1930 the film rights were sold to Metro-Goldwyn-Mayer. It was used to launch the career of MGM's new operatic star, Miss Grace Moore. Her co-star was Metropolitan Opera star, Lawrence Tibbett. MGM altered the plot from the French Revolution to the Russian Revolution of 1917 and some of the original songs were dropped from the film score. The picture was not a success and did not help the careers of its two stars. Buster Keaton and Nat Pendleton both were featured in the MacDonald-Eddy version when production started, but as the film progressed their parts were taken out.

New York Daily News—Wanda Hale

*** (Three Stars). Reunited after a two year vacation, Jeanette MacDonald and Nelson Eddy are thrilling fans at the Capitol Theatre by their renditions of the ever-popular Romberg-Hammerstein melodies in Metro-Goldwyn-Mayer's remake of *New Moon.* The audience expressed hearty approval of the reunion of these two musical comedy stars by more enthusiastic applause after they duet-ed than after an individual performance. Though they were by no means unappreciative of the solos.

I'll See You Again

Bitter Sweet

Technicolor
A Metro-Goldwyn-Mayer Picture   1940

Produced by Victor Saville. Directed by W. S. Van Dyke. Screenplay by Lesser Samuels; based on the play by Noel Coward. Produced on the Broadway stage by Florenz Ziegfeld and Arch Selwyn. Photography by Oliver T. Marsh and Allan Davey. Technicolor director, Natalie Kalmus; associate, Henri Jaffa. Musical direction by Herbert Stothart. Vocal and orchestral arrangements by Ken Darby and Murray Cutter. Musical presentation by Merrill Pye. Dance direction by Ernst Matray. Recording director, Douglas Shearer. Art direction by Cedric Gibbons. Set decorations by Edwin B. Willis. Gowns by Adrian. Men's costumes by Gile Steele. Hair styles for Miss MacDonald by Sidney Guilaroff. Makeup created by Jack Dawn. Film editor, Harold F. Kress.   94 minutes.

Songs "Zigeuner," "If You Could Only Come with Me," and "Kiss Me," music and lyrics by Noel Coward. "I'll See You Again," "Dear Little Cafe," "What Is Love," "Ladies of the Town," "Tokay," "Love In Any Language," music by Noel Coward, special lyrics by Gus Kahn.

With Lynne Carver

CAST
Sarah Millick, JEANETTE MacDONALD; *Carl Linden,* NELSON EDDY; *Baron Von Tranisch,* GEORGE SANDERS; *Lord Shayne,* Ian Hunter; *Max,* Felix Bressart; *Harry Daventry,* Edward Ashley; *Dolly,* Lynne Carver; *Jane,* Diana Lewis; *Sophie,* Veda Ann Borg; *Ernst,* Curt Bois; *Mrs. Millick,* Fay Holden; *Roger,* Dalies Frantz; *Herr Wyler,* Charles Judels; *Herr Schlick,* Sig Rumann; *Market Keeper,* Herman Bing; *Lady Daventry,* Janet Beecher.

With George Sanders

With a Hungarian gypsy chorus presenting a song production of "Zigeuner"

SYNOPSIS

In a prologue to the main story of *Bitter Sweet*, Roger, a young artist, is in despair of ever marrying his sweetheart. To encourage him in the belief that love conquers all, his client, Lord Shayne, takes him to meet a charming seventy-year-old lady, Sarah Millick, who had been a famous singer. Roger then learns the story of her life: On the eve of her marriage to Harry Daventry, a young Englishman, Victorian belle Sarah Millick scandalized her family and friends by her unnaturally excited conduct at a ball in London. She then eloped to Vienna with her singing teacher, Carl Linden. There they lived in poverty—but happily—among Carl's friends. Carl's hope of selling an operetta he had written to Herr Wyler, impresario, had met with no response, but fortunes changed when Sarah won the attention of young Lord Shayne and his gambling opponent, Baron Von Tranisch, of the Imperial Cavalry. Shayne believes that Sarah's singing brought him luck. Von Tranisch had a more personal romantic interest. He instructed Herr Schlick to hire Sarah as an entertainer in his Vienna Cafe where Carl was to lead the orchestra. When Von Tranisch paid unwelcome attentions to Sarah, she resisted. But again Von Tranisch became offensive. Carl found himself forced into a duel which he had no hope of winning, and Von Tranisch ran him through. Carl died in Sarah's arms. She found a new hope, however, in the fact that her friend and later benefactor, Lord Shayne, persuaded Wyler to produce the operetta with her as star. Thus Carl's music lived on through her singing, and every time she sang his music she felt that he was with her. In the epiloque, Roger, inspired by the story, finds himself with a new sense of values and joyfully goes to meet the girl he now plans to marry.

COMMENTS

Bitter Sweet was filmed in England in 1933 with Anna Neagle and Fernand Gravet in the two leads. Filmed in beautiful Technicolor this time, the new version was hailed as another *Maytime*. This time it was George Sanders' turn to play the villain, killing Nelson in the swiftest screen duel on record. The lovely music of Noel Coward was memorable, and the film fared well at the box office.

Time

Noel Coward's romantic story of old Vienna with its enchanting music and background comes to the screen in the most exquisite Technicolor yet seen. In fact, the color, especially in the beautiful copper and white ballet number

With Ian Hunter

steals the honors, which is no small achievement considering the beauty of Jeanette MacDonald and the singing of Nelson Eddy. George Sanders plays the villain as only George Sanders can. It's a pleasure just to watch Mr. Sanders in action. Diana Lewis is cute as the lisping gold-digger. The songs "I'll See You Again" and "Zigeuner" are beautifully sung by this popular screen team.

Variety

Bitter Sweet is a super-elaborate production in Technicolor, providing a visual-appeal background for mounting of the fetching Noel Coward songs, in his highly successful operetta, delivered in solo and duet by Jeanette MacDonald and Nelson Eddy. It's now chiefly eye-and-ear entertainment, with the original sentimental charm and romance of the stage version missing. For music lovers and the MacDonald-Eddy adherents, picture is a musical treat that will hit the gait of previous releases of the singing team.

With Gene Raymond and Patrick O'Moore

Smilin' Through
Technicolor
A Metro-Goldwyn-Mayer Picture   1941

Produced by Victor Saville. Directed by Frank Borzage. Screenplay by Donald Ogden Stewart and John Balderston; based on the play by Jane Cowl and Jane Murfin. Photography by Leonard Smith. Technicolor consultant, Natalie Kalmus; associate, Henri Jaffa. Musical director, Herbert Stothart. Recording director, Douglas Shearer. Art director, Cedric Gibbons; associate, Daniel B. Cathcart. Set decorations by Edwin B. Willis. Special effects by Warren Newcombe. Montage effects by Peter Ballbusch. Gowns by Adrian. Men's costumes by Gile Steele. Makeup by Jack Dawn. Film editor, Frank Sullivan.   100 minutes.

Songs "Smilin Through," music and lyrics by Arthur A. Penn. "Just a Little Love, a Little Kiss," music by Adrian Ross, lyrics by Lao Silesu. "Ouvre Coeur," by Bizet. "The Kerry Dance," music and lyrics by J.L. Molloy. "Hope and Glory," music by Sir Edward Elgar, lyrics by A. C. Blason. "Drink to Me Only with Thine Eyes," Music-Anonymous. Lyrics by Ben Jonson with special musical arrangements by Herbert Stothart. "There's a Long Long Trail," music by Z.O. Elliot, lyrics by Stoddard King.

With Brian Aherne

CAST
Kathleen/Moonyean Clare, JEANETTE MacDONALD; *Sir John Carteret,* BRIAN AHERNE; *Kenneth Wayne/ Jeremy Wayne,* GENE RAYMOND; *Reverend Owen Harding,* Ian Hunter; *Ellen,* Frances Robinson; *Willie,* Patrick O'Moore; *Charles (Batman),* Eric Lonsdale; *Kathleen (as a child),* Jackie Horner; *Sexton,* David Clyde; *Dowager,* Frances Carson; *Woman,* Ruth Rickaby.

With Brian Aherne and Ian Hunter

SYNOPSIS

In 1897, Queen Victoria's Jubilee Year, Sir John Carteret is haunted by the shadow and the memory of lovely Moonyean Clare, the Irish girl he was to wed almost thirty years before. She has been taken from him by the frenzied jealousy of a disappointed suitor, Jeremy Wayne. At home, the Rev. Owen Harding and Ellen, the housekeeper, have sent for Kathleen, Moonyean's five year old orphaned niece. At first Sir John resents the child, but the tiny Kathleen soon wins his heart. She grows into young womanhood beloved by him and Owen. Meeting Kenneth Wayne, newly arrived from America to join the British Army, it is love at first sight for the now grown Kathleen. When Sir John learns of this, he turns into a stern, unbending man. Then Kathleen learns it was Jeremy Wayne, Kenneth's father, who rushed to the wedding to kill his rival, while Moonyean, protecting John, was herself killed.

Kathleen tries to forget Kenneth as he leaves, but their love is too great. Kenneth returns from the war greatly changed. He declares he no longer loves Kathleen and is returning to America. Heartbroken, she determines to leave Sir John's house forever. What she doesn't know is that Kenneth, who has been wounded, refuses to be a burden to her. Owen learns the truth and informs Kathleen. It is then that Sir John realizes he has lost both Kathleen and Moonyean, through his hate. He sends Kathleen to Kenneth. In the midst of a chess game with Owen, Sir John, who has cherished Moonyean in his heart for 50 years, falls limp. With the strain of the haunting "Smilin' Through," he meets his separated bride, and their love culminates in the wedding that was denied them on earth.

With Brian Aherne

With Ian Hunter and Brian Aherne

COMMENTS

Smilin' Through was performed on the Broadway stage in 1919 with Jane Cowl the play's co-author. It was filmed in 1922 with Norma Talmadge and again in 1932 with Norma Shearer, Leslie Howard and Fredric March.

Los Angeles Examiner—Louella O. Parsons

The "third" edition of *Smilin' Through* comes to moviegoers with the addition of enchanting music and Technicolor which brings out the red in Jeanette MacDonald's hair and gives her a breathtaking beauty . . . Jeanette MacDonald fans will undoubtably list this as one of her outstanding pictures.

Metro-Goldwyn-Mayer's *The Lion's Roar*

Those who have bathed their eyes in the romance of Moonyean Clare will be interested to know that in this moondrenched incarnation, the director, Frank Borzage, has rendered us a musical version starring the incomparable Jeanette MacDonald. And co-starring the logical choice, Brian Aherne as Sir John Carteret. Gene Raymond and Ian Hunter must be emphasized, for they are major curves in a rounded cast. Many of us are in love with the spirit of *Smilin' Through*. Many more of us will be when we see and hear Jeanette's Moonyean in perfected Technicolor.

With Rise Stevens and Nigel Bruce

The Chocolate Soldier
A Metro-Goldwyn-Mayer Picture   1941

Produced by Victor Saville. Directed by Roy Del Ruth. Screenplay by Keith Winter and Leonard Lee; additional screenplay contributions by Ernest Vajda and Claudine West; based on the play *The Guardsman* by Ferenc Molnar. Photography by Karl Freund. Musical adaptation and direction by Herbert Stothart. Musical presentation by Merrill Pye. Music by Oscar Straus. Original lyrics by Rudolph Bernauer and Leopold Jacobson. English lyrics by Stanislaus Stange. Additional music and lyrics by Bronislau Kaper and Gus Kahn. Dances created by Ernst Matray. Art direction by Cedric Gibbons; associate, John Detlie. Set direction by Edwin B. Willis. Recording director, Douglas Shearer. Gowns by Adrian. Film editor, James Newcome.   102 minutes.

Songs   "While My Lady Sleeps," music by Bronislau Kaper, lyrics by Gus Kahn. "Song of the Flea," by Mussorgsky. "Evening Star," by Wagner.   "Seek the Spy," music by Oscar Straus, lyrics by Stanislaus Stange, addi-

tional lyrics by Gus Kahn. "My Heart at Thy Sweet Voice," by Saint-Saens. "Mon Coeur," by Bizet. "Ti-Ra-La-La," music by Oscar Straus, lyrics by Stanislaus Stange, additional lyrics by Gus Kahn. "My Hero," music by Oscar Straus, lyrics by Stanislaus Stange. "Thank the Lord the War Is Over," music by Oscar Straus, lyrics by Stanislaus Stange. "Sympathy," music by Oscar Straus, lyrics by Stanislaus Stange. "The Chocolate Soldier," music by Oscar Straus, lyrics by Stanislaus Stange. "Forgive," music by Oscar Straus, lyrics by Stanislaus Stange.

CAST
Karl Lang, NELSON EDDY; *Maria Lanyi*, RISE STEVENS; *Bernard Fischer*, Nigel Bruce; *Mme. Helene*, Florence Bates; *Liesel*, Nydia Westman; *Klementov*, Charles Judels; *Captain Masakroff*, Jack Lipson; *Magda*, Dorothy Gilmore; *Anton*, Max Barwyn; *Waiter*, Leon Belasco; *Emile*, Sig Arno; *Messenger Boy*, Dave Willock.

With Rise Stevens and Florence Bates

With Rise Stevens and Nigel Bruce

SYNOPSIS

Karl Lang and his wife, Maria, are the singing hits of Vienna. However, Karl is extremely jealous of the flirtatious Maria and decides to masquerade as a Russian guardsman in order to test his wife's loyalty. The guardsman has himself introduced in a Cafe as a new singer and directs all his songs directly to Maria, oblivious of the other diners. Maria agrees to receive the guardsman who proceeds to make violent love to her. Upset by the intensity of his ardor she angrily orders him to leave only to tell him that Karl will be out that evening. Maria's vacillating between rejecting the "Russian's" advances and encouraging him, keeps Karl in constant turmoil so that he can no longer play the dual role. At a performance of *The Chocolate Soldier*, he retires to change for their next number together. However, instead of dressing for the role, he assumes his Russian costume and strides onto the stage singing in the bass he's been using as the Russian. Maria, surprised, completes the number with him during which she tells Karl that she's known all along about the masquerade and declares her love for him. Karl is convinced and the two leave the stage arm in arm to the final notes of "My Hero."

With Rise Stevens

With Rise Stevens, Florence Bates

COMMENTS

As early as 1935, MGM tried to screen *The Chocolate Soldier* with Maurice Chevalier and Grace Moore, but Chevalier refused to take second billing to Miss Moore. He cancelled his long term MGM contract after making only one film. Rise Stevens, the lovely Metropolitan Opera star, made her film debut in this film. Bernard Shaw's *Arms and the Man* is nominally the plot of *The Chocolate Soldier*. In this instance MGM and Shaw could not come to terms. So the studio, which owned screen rights to Molnar's *The Guardsman*, substituted the material from the latter, and the results were felicitous.

Variety

Both Eddy and Miss Stevens are in fine fettle. Eddy, does a remarkable piece of impersonation as the Russian singer, perhaps his finest endeavor as an actor. The characterization is alive with humor.

Columnist Jimmy Fidler
Nelson Eddy in *The Chocolate Soldier*—best performance.
A great singer proves he's become a fine actor.

I Married an Angel

A Metro-Goldwyn-Mayer Picture   1942

Produced by Hunt Stromberg. Directed by W.S. Van Dyke. Screenplay by Anita Loos; based on the stage play by Vaszary Jones. Produced on the Broadway stage by Dwight Wiman. Photography by Ray June. Dance direction by Ernst Matray. Recording director, Douglas Shearer. Art director, Cedric Gibbons; Associate art directors, John S. Dietlie and Motley. Special effects, Arnold Gillespie and Warren Newcombe. Costumes by Motley. Gowns by Kalloch, Hair styles by Sidney Guilaroff. Makeup created by Jack Dawn. Film editor, Conrad A. Nervig.   84 minutes.

Songs "I Married an Angel," "Spring Is Here," "I'll Tell the Man in the Street," "End of a Dream," "Paris Honeymoon Suite," "The Guests Meet Willie's Bride," "Paris in Spring," "A Twinkle in Your Eye," "Surprise Party," "An Angel Appears," and "Brigitta Arrives at the Night Club." Music by Richard Rodgers. Lyrics by Lorenz Hart; additional lyrics by Bob Wright and Chet Forrest.

CAST
Anna/Brigitta, JEANETTE MacDONALD; *Count Palaffi,* NELSON EDDY; *Peter,* Edward Everett Horton; *Peggy,* Binnie Barnes; *"Whiskers,"* Reginald Owen; *Baron Szigethy,* Douglass Dumbrille; *Marika,* Mona Maris; *Iren,* Inez Cooper; *Zinski,* Leonid Kinskey; *Polly,* Anne Jeffreys; *Dolly,* Marion Rosamond; *Sufi,* Janis Carter.

SYNOPSIS

At his birthday party, the dashing young Count Willie Palaffi, is forced to dance with drab Anna Zader, a stenographer in his bank. He finally excuses himself, and in his own room falls asleep, dreaming that a beautiful angel comes through the window on a cloud. The angel is Anna, wearing a beautiful robe complete with wings and halo, and Willie realizes he must marry her. In his fantasy the two are off on their honeymoon. Anna wants to leave her husband the first night to sleep on a cloud but he persuades her to remain, and the next morning she is minus her wings. Willie now receives word that the news of his elopement has reached Budapest and that there will be a run on the bank unless he returns. Post-haste the two return to Budapest, where Willie decides to dispel the rumors and prove he is married to a wonderful woman by giving a banquet for all his stodgy business associates. But at the banquet, Anna adheres so strictly to the truth and tells her husband's business secrets with such alacrity that the guests depart in amazement and there is a run on the bank. At this conjuncture Willie awakens and heaves a great sigh of relief that it has only been a dream. He returns to the party where he discovers poor little Anna just where he left her. The dream has only taken three minutes.

With Mona Maris

With Raphael Storm   With Binnie Barnes

COMMENTS

Louis B. Mayer was much irked at Paramount's signing Vera Zorina after MGM bought the rights to *I Married An Angel*. Paramount refused to lend her to MGM, although they did loan her to Warner Bros. for *On Your Toes*. Nelson was originally intended to make *We Were Dancing* with Norma Shearer and a song was to be included for him. He also tested for *Idiot's Delight,* but the role went to Clark Gable. Although he and Shearer had qualities that interested Mayer, as indicated by their test, he kept in the back of his mind the idea of using them together and *We Were Dancing* was decided as the film. However, when Zorina was unavailable for *I Married An Angel* Jeanette and Nelson won the leads. Both felt they were unsuited to their roles in this film but both tried very hard to make the picture work. The disappointment of *I Married An Angel* at the box-office must not be charged to Jeanette and Nelson but to Louis B. Mayer, since the decision for them to do it was his and his alone and each opposed it, singularly and together. *I Married An Angel* was the last film that both Jeanette and Nelson did together.

Photopolay

Much below the standard of MGM's singing stars Nelson Eddy and Jeanette MacDonald is this bit of trivia taken from the paper thin stage play of several seasons ago. Neither star is given songs that come even near meeting his vocal ability. Because this pair is your favorite and you approve them in anything, we give this our one-check blessing and hope for better things next time. Your reviewer says: Two artists in search of a good story.

Daily Variety

While *I Married An Angel* has it's production merits and it's moments of engaging comedy, music, and decided pictorial entertainment, it does not in general indicate more than average returns from the majority of the situations.

With Mona Maris, Rafaella Ottiano, and Tyler Brooke

With Robert Young

Cairo

A Metro-Goldwyn-Mayer Picture   1942

Produced by Metro-Goldwyn-Mayer. Directed by Major W. S. Van Dyke. Screenplay by John McClain; based upon an idea by Ladislas Fodor. Photographed by Ray June. Musical score by Herbert Stothart. Musical conductor, Georgie Stoll. Dance direction by Sammy Lee. Recording director, Douglas Shearer. Art directions by Cedric Gibbons; associate, Lyle Wheeler. Set directions by Edwin S. Willis; associate, Richard Pefferle. Gowns by Kalloch. Film editor, James E. Newcomb.   101 minutes.

Songs "The Maid from Cadiz," music by Leo Delibes, lyrics by Alfred De Musset. "Buds Won't Bud," "A Woman Without a Man," music by Harold Arlen, lyrics by E. Y. Harburg. "The Waltz Is Over," and "Keep the Light Burning Bright in the Harbor," music by Arthur Schwartz, lyrics by E. Y. Harburg. "Waiting for the Robert E. Lee," music by Lewis F. Muir, lyrics by L. Wolfe Gilbert.

CAST

Marcia Warren, JEANETTE MacDONALD; *Homer Smith,* ROBERT YOUNG; *Cleona Jones,* ETHEL WATERS; *Philo Cobson,* Reginald Owen; *O. H. P. Beggs,* Grant Mitchell; *Teutonic Gentleman,* Lionel Atwill; *Ahmed Ben Hassen,* Eduardo Ciannelli; *Mrs. Morrison,* Mona Barrie; *Ludwig,* Mitchell Lewis; *Hector,* Dooley Wilson; *Bernie,* Larry Nunn; *Colonel Woodhue,* Dennis Hoey; *Strange Man,* Rhys Williams; *Mme. Laruga,* Cecil Cunningham; *Bartender,* Harry Worth; *Alfred,* Frank Richards.

Jeanette sings a medley of songs: "Avalon," "I Want to Go Back to Michigan," "To a Wild Rose," "Land of the Sky Blue Waters," "Beautiful Ohio," and "Home Sweet Home." Aria from "Figaro," (duet) sung by Jeanette and Ethel Waters.

With Ethel Waters

SYNOPSIS

Homer Smith, a war correspondent leaves for Cairo on a news assignment. Homer's ship is torpedoed somewhere in the Mediterranean and he is shipwrecked on a raft in the middle of the sea. A fellow passenger, Philo Cobson, floats alongside the raft and is rescued by Homer. The two finally reach land (the Libyan Desert), but they are forced to separate when they hear a troop of German soldiers approaching. It is Cobson who suggests they part.

On the confidential information that he is a British agent, Cobson, imparts certain military secrets to Homer, and asks him to approach a certain Mrs. Morrison in Cairo. Homer will know her because she always orders a special cocktail. At the Empire Hotel, an attractive woman approaches the bar and orders a cocktail. It is Mrs. Morrison. Homer passes on the information and is told by Mrs. Morrison that the leader of the Nazi "Big Six" is none other than the beautiful American movie star, Marcia Warren, who is in Cairo entertaining the British troops there. Homer is convinced of the truth when he sees Marcia and her maid, Cleona, exchange a series of mysterious signs. Homer learns that an Arab named Ahmed has devised a devilish plot whereby, through remote control, a ship can be bombed by a plane via radio controls. Homer, trapped, drops $100 bills along the sand. Sure enough, the bills do lead Marcia and the bonafide British Intelligence Officers to the pyramid. Suddenly, half afraid to voice her suggestions, Marcia mentions the bills and their slang name—"C" notes. Her clear, bell-like high C rings out into the night. She's hit the secret. Slowly the pyramid moves, it opens. There revealed is the hideout of the "Big Six." They've arrived just in time to save Homer from crashing with the bomb-laden plane into a transport and it's precious cargo of American soldiers.

COMMENTS

Cairo was planned and partly filmed in color but released completely as a black and white film. There is a very good line in the film: Robert Young asks Jeanette where she comes from. Jeanette replies, "California." He admits that he also comes from California. Robert says to her, "Have you ever been in San Francisco?" She replies, "Yes, once with Gable and Tracy."

The New York Times—Bosley Crowther
If MGM's *Cairo* which opened at the Capitol yesterday

were one-half as entertaining as every current news dispatch with that dateline, it would be the most thrilling picture to come along in three years. But, unfortunately, it isn't, and it is the embarrassment of Metro that it has nothing tacked to that title at this time but a muddle of melodrama, music, and farce. . . . And who have we in it but Jeanette MacDonald playing an American movie queen in Cairo, and Robert Young playing a dopey newsman who suspects her of being a Nazi spy. Every so often time is taken and Miss MacDonald tosses off a full-voiced song. And now and again Lionel Atwill, Mona Barrie and Eduardo Ciannelli lay serious plots. But mostly the screen is agitated by Miss MacDonald and Mr. Young being coy, each suspecting the other with not very humorous consequence. That is the fault of the picture. It's farce is exceedingly flat, both in conception and execution.

Photoplay
"Oh, dear, we're afraid this isn't very good and Jeanette MacDonald did so need a strong picture after several weak ones in a row. But it does have it's moments of fun with Bob Young, an American correspondent in Cairo, and Jeanette, an American singer, the dupe of Nazi sympathizers. The way Bob and Jeanette chase each other around is a caution. Jeanette sings beautifully. Ethel Waters is superb as the maid. Your reviewer says: "Well, they meant well.""

The Phantom of the Opera

Technicolor
A Universal Picture   1943

With Susanna Foster

Produced by George Waggner. Directed by Arthur Lubin. First assistant director, Charles Gould. Dialogue director, Joan Hathaway. Screenplay by Eric Taylor and Samuel Hoffenstein; based on the novel by Gaston Leroux. Adaptation by John Jacoby. Photography by Hal Mohr and W. Howard Greene. Color consultant, Natalie Kalmus. Musical direction by Edward Ward. Orchestrations by Harold Zweifel and Arthur Schutt. Choral direction by William Tyroler. Opera sequences staged by William Von Wymetal and Lester Horton. Operatic score and libretto by Edward Ward and George Waggner. Sound director, Bernard B. Brown. Technician, Joe Laepis. Art direction by John B. Goodman and Alexander Golitzen. Set decorations by R. A. Gausman and Ira S. Webb. Costumes by Vera West. Hair styles by Emily Moore. Makeup by Jack Pierce. Film editor, Russell Schoengarth.   92 minutes.

Songs "Lullaby of the Bells," music by Edward Ward, lyrics by George Waggner.

Music that was used in the film were scenes and arias from *Martha* (Von Flotow) excerpts from Acts III and IV. "L'Amour Et Gloire" was based on Chopin's music. "Le Prince Masque de la Caucasie (The Masked Prince of the Caucasus) was based on Tchaikovsky themes, from his Symphony No. 4 in F. Minor. "Nocturne In E Flat" was based on music by Chopin.

CAST

Anatole Garron, NELSON EDDY; *Christine DuBois,* SUSANNA FOSTER; *Erique Claudin,* CLAUDE RAINS; *Raoul,* Edgar Barrier; *Signor Ferretti,* Leo Carrillo; *Biancarolli,* Jane Farrar; *Amiot,* J. Edward Bromberg; *Lecours,* Fritz Feld; *Villeneuve,* Frank Puglia; *Vercheres,* Steven Geray; *Christine's Aunt,* Barbara Everest; *Gerard,* Hume Cronyn; *Lizst,* Fritz Leiber; *Russian Princess,* Nicki Andre; *Landlady,* Kate Lawson; *Pleyel,* Miles Mander; *Doctor,* Walter Stahl; *Desjardines,* Paul Marion; *Christine's Maid,* Rosina Galli; *Ferretti's Maid,* Belle Mitchell; *Pleyel's Secretary,* Renee Carson.

With Jane Farrar,
Susanna Foster,
Hume Cronyn and
Edgar Barrier

Claude Rains

With Steven Geray, Hume Cronyn and Edgar Barrier

SYNOPSIS

Violinist Erique Claudin, a sensitive musician is so incensed when music publisher Pleyel refuses to listen to his piano concerto, a work that he spent years composing, that when he hears his concerto played in the publishing office and believes it's being pirated, he kills the publisher in a mad fit of temperament. Pleyel's mistress-secretary, standing helplessly by, throws a tray full of liquid acid in Claudin's face in order to stop him. Driven insane by the pain, Claudin escapes from the office and crawls into a sewer. Later, in the catacombs under the Paris Opera House, he takes refuge while divising a plan to seek revenge on all those he believes have slighted him.

Wearing a mask to hide his horribly scarred face, and a cloak stolen from the costume department of the opera company, Claudin begins a reign of terror among members of the company who came to regard him as "The Phantom." He murders divas ruthlessly so that a young understudy, Christine DuBois, to whom he has become attached, may have an opportunity to sing the star roles, thereby gaining personal fame. The terror is investigated by a detective of the Sureté, Raoul Daubert, who becomes smitten with Christine. He is the rival of the opera company's baritone, Anatole Garron, for her affections. When Daubert, thwarts one of Claudin's attempts at murder and terror, Claudin retaliates by sawing the suspension chains of a gigantic crystal chandelier that hangs above the orchestra seats of the opera house, and sends it crashing onto the audience on a night when the house is filled to capacity. During the panic that follows, Claudin kidnaps Christine and takes her to the catacombs. He tells her he intends for them to live there together, playing music on a piano while Christine sings to him. Her terror at his proposal is absolute. Daubert and Garron discover the entrance to the catacombs through a secret passage, arriving just in time to save Christine's life. She has unmasked the "Phantom." Raoul shoots at Claudin and the concussion dislodges the catacomb supports. Claudin is killed in the cave-in, while Daubert and Garron come to Christine's aid and bring her to safety.

COMMENTS

The Phantom of the Opera won three Academy Awards for cinematography, art direction and interior decoration. *The Phantom of the Opera*, which no one seems to recall, starred Nelson Eddy. Whatever reason Universal had to induce him to color his hair and add a moustache for him to look as much like Edgar Barrier, his romantic rival for Susanna Foster, was certainly a grave mistake. Edward Ward composed a memorable refrain entitled "Lullaby of the Bells." In selecting the musical score for the operatic sequences, Ward chose a single standard opera, the third act from "Martha," and wrote the other two acts himself.

The Pacific Coast Musician—Vernon Steele

Susanna Foster, in this opus, emerges as one of the most beautiful voices and delightful singers on the screen. . . . Nelson Eddy is a vastly improved singer and likes the music in *Phantom of the Opera* so well that he is arranging to use part of it on his forthcoming recital tour.

Look

The silent film, forerunner of our present "Frankenstein" and "Wolf Man" blood-splatters was strong meat. But this version, less creepy, has probably wider appeal . . . Nelson Eddy sings magnificently as the French baritone. Just by keeping pace, Susanna Foster, the understudy, insures herself a shining future. And although Claude Rains' phantom may disappoint some old Chaney fans, it is only because there is less ham in Rains, more actor.

With Susanna Foster and Edgar Barrier

Knickerbocker Holiday

Producers Corporation of America—A United
Artists Release 1944

Produced and directed by Harry Joe Brown. Screenplay by
David Boehm and Rowland Leigh; based on the musical
play, book, and lyrics by Maxwell Anderson. Photography by Phil Tannura. Musical direction, Jacques Samas-
soud. Musical score by Werner Heymann. Film editor,
John F. Link.   85 minutes.

Songs "The New Governor of Amsterdam," "There's
Nowhere to Go but Up," "Holiday," "Love Has Made
This Such a Lovely Day," "Zuyder Zee," "September
Song," "The Jail Song," "One More Smile," "The One
Indispensible Man," "Be Not Hasty, Gentle Maiden,"
"Sing Out," and "Let's Make Tomorrow Today." Music
by Kurt Weill. Lyrics by Maxwell Anderson.

CAST
Brom Broeck, NELSON EDDY; *Peter Stuyvesant,*
CHARLES COBURN; *Tina,* CONSTANCE DOWLING;
Tienhoven, Ernest Cossart; *Ten Pin,* Johnnie Scat Davis;
Ulda, Shelley Winters; *Tamany,* Richard Hale; *Big Mus-
cle,* Glenn Strange; *Poffenburgh,* Fritz Feld; *Roosevelt,*
Otto Kruger; *De Vries,* Percival Vivian; *Renssaler,*
Charles Judels; *De Pyster,* Ferdinand Munier; *Schermer-
horn,* Percy Kilbride; *Town Crier,* Chester Conklin;
Guard, Ralph Dunn; *Barmaid,* Dorothy Granger and Car-
men Amaya Troupe.

With Fritz Feld, Charles Coburn and Constance Dowling

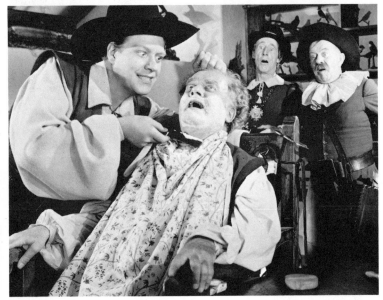

With Charles Coburn, Constance Dowling and Ernest Cossart

SYNOPSIS

In the days of 1650, when Manhattan was known as New Amsterdam and was under Dutch rule, Brom Broeck, a young, freedom-loving newspaper publisher, doesn't object to speaking his mind and putting his thoughts into bold-faced print. Whilst carrying on a romance with the daughter of one of the city's councilmen, he fights the undemocratic rule of Governor Peter "Peg-Leg" Stuyvesant and the city fathers. Stuyvesant jails Broeck for his advanced opinions and then, although he is an old man, Stuyvesant goes on the make for Brom's pretty sweetheart.

Stuyvesant is persuaded to pardon Brom and to get rid of him sends him out into the wilderness to unite the colonists. Simultaneously, he plots to convert the township's many corruptions to his own profit, but Brom convinces him that such actions will not stand well with posterity— Stuyvesant reforms in his fashion, relinquishing the girl to Brom.

COMMENTS

Nelson produced the film version of *Knickerbocker Holiday*. He had invested in the Broadway production that starred Walter Huston in 1938. The film didn't do too well at the box office. Nelson did not cast himself to best advantage since the Charles Coburn role is the main character and has the only memorable song. Time hasn't helped the film at all. Even the film's main attraction, Coburn singing "September Song," leaves more than a little to be desired. Burt Lancaster did a better job with it on stage in the Los Angeles production than Coburn did in the film, which is indeed faint praise. Beautiful Constance Dowling made a lovely Tina.

The New York Times

Nelson Eddy carries his musical chores as he always does, but his attempted acting of the role of the harumscarum young firebrand, Brom Broeck, is too much of a drain on his vitality. . . . All in all one gets the impression that *Knickerbocker Holiday* wasn't much a holiday for those who made it, and likely is not a hilarious holiday for those who see it.

With Ernest Cossart (in chair), Percy Kilbride and Chester Conklin

Follow the Boys
A Universal Picture 1944

Produced by Charles K. Feldman. Associate producer, Albert L. Rockett. Directed by Eddie Sutherland. Assistant director, Howard Christie. Original screenplay by Lou Breslow and Gertrude Purcell. Photography by David Abel. Special photography by John P. Fulton. Musical director, Leigh Harline. Musical production numbers staged and devised by George Hale. Soldiers In Grease Paint'' number by Joe Schoenfeld. Recording director, Bernard B. Brown. Technician, Robert Pritchard. Art direction by John B. Goodman and Harold H. MacArthur. Set directions by Russell A. Gausman and Ira S. Webb. Gowns by Vera West. Miss Zorina's jewelry by Lacritz. Miss Zorina's gowns by Howard Greer. Film editor, Fred R. Feitshans, Jr.   122 minutes.

Songs   "The Bigger the Army and Navy," music and lyrics by Jack Yellen. "Some of these Days," music and lyrics by Shelton Brooks. "Liebestraum," by Liszt. "I'll Get By," music and lyrics by Roy Turk and Fred E. Ahlert. "I'll Walk Alone," music and lyrics by Jule Styne and Sammy Cahn. "Mad About Him Blues," music and lyrics by Larry Marks and Dick Charles. "Good Night," music and lyrics by Leo Wood, Con Conrad, and Irving Bibo. "Furlough Fling," music and lyrics by Charles Weintraub and Frank Davenport. "Shoo Shoo Baby," music and lyrics by Phil Moore. "Swing Low, Sweet Chariot," music and lyrics by Henry Thacher Burleigh. "Sweet Georgia Brown," music and lyrics by Ben Bernie and Casey Pinkard. "Is You Is, Or Is You Ain't My Baby," music and lyrics by Louis Jordan and Billy Austin. "Tonight," music and lyrics by Kermit Goel and Walter Donaldson. "I Feel a Song Coming On," music and lyrics by Jimmy McHugh, Dorothy Fields, and George Oppenheimer. "The House I Live In," music and lyrics by Earl Robinson and Lewis Allen. "A Better Day Is Comin," music and lyrics by Jule Styne and Sammy Cahn. "Merriment," music and lyrics by Augustin Costellon Sabicas. "Kittens with Their Mittens Laced," music and lyrics by Inez James and Sidney Miller.

Singing, "Beyond the Blue Horizon"

With John Meredith, singing, "I'll See You in My Dreams"

CAST

Tony West, GEORGE RAFT; *Gloria Vance,* VERA ZO-RINA; *Nick West,* Charley Grapewin; *Kitty West,* Grace McDonald; *Louie Fairweather,* Charles Butterworth; *Walter Bruce,* George Macready; *Annie,* Elizabeth Patterson; *William Barnett,* Theodore Von Eltz; *Dr. Henderson,* Regis Toomey; *Laura,* Ramsay Ames; *Chic Doyle,* Frank Jenks and Martha O'Driscoll and Maxie Rosenbloom.

Appearing in the Hollywood Victory Committee sequence
SUSANNA FOSTER; MARIA MONTEZ; LOUISE ALLBRITTON; ROBERT PAIGE; ALAN CURTIS; LON CHANEY; GLORIA JEAN; ANDY DEVINE; TURHAN BEY; EVELYN ANKERS; NOAH BEERY, JR; GALE SONDERGAARD; PETER COE; NIGEL BRUCE; THOMAS GOMEZ; LOIS COLLIER; SAMUEL S. HINDS; AND LOUISE BEAVERS.

GUEST STARS (In Order of Appearance)
JEANETTE MacDONALD; ORSON WELLES; MARLENE DIETRICH; DINAH SHORE; DONALD O'CONNOR; PEGGY RYAN; W.C. FIELDS; THE ANDREWS SISTERS; ARTUR RUBINSTEIN; CARMEN AMAYA And Her Company; SOPHIE TUCKER; DELTA RHYTHM BOYS; LEONARD GAUTIER'S BRICKLAYERS; TED LEWIS AND HIS BAND; FREDDIE SLACK AND HIS ORCHESTRA; CHARLIE SPIVAK AND HIS ORCHESTRA and LOUIS JORDAN AND HIS ORCHESTRA.

Jeanette MacDonald's sequence occurs in a military hospital while visiting wounded servicemen. During the visit she stages an impromptu concert and sings "I'll See You in My Dreams" to a blind soldier, and sings "Beyond the Blue Horizon" to a large crowd on a stage outdoors. Her footage runs approximately 14½ minutes. "I'll See You in My Dreams," music and lyrics by Gus Kahn and Isham Jones. "Beyond the Blue Horizon," music

and lyrics by Richard Whiting, W. Frank Harling and Leo Robin.

SYNOPSIS

After the death of vaudeville, the "Three Wests" try burlesque and fail. The act splits up and Tony heads for Hollywood where he is partnered with Gloria Vance. They are a success and all goes well until Pearl Harbor. Tony tries to enlist but is rejected. Tony soon begins to see the need to entertain the servicemen and his idea grows into the Hollywood Victory Committee with the motion picture industry pitching in to make the program a success. Gloria and Tony, who are wed, become estranged. Tony takes a unit of stars on the first trip abroad and when the ship is torpedoed Tony dies heroically after learning that Gloria is to have his child. Later, Gloria realizes the full meaning of Tony's devotion to this cause and volunteers to "follow the boys."

COMMENTS

Universal called on their many stars to guest star in *Follow the Boys.* It was nice seeing the stars that appeared in the Hollywood Victory Committee sequence and also the stars appearing in doing bits of music, song, and dance.

The New York Times—Bosley Crowther

As evidence of the sort of entertainment which is being generously provided for the troops, this two-hour melange of variety is probably a credible display. But as orderly screen composition it hasn't the slightest claim . . . Perhaps there are plenty of people who can take entertainment this way—with performers just standing before microphones and tossing it out loud and long. But it makes for cheap screen entertainment—and hardly a tribute to the players it represents.

200

With Walt Disney

Make Mine Music
A Walt Disney Production—Released by RKO
Pictures   1946

Production supervisor, Joe Grant. Directors, Jack Kinney, Clyde Geronimi, Hamilton Luske, Robert Cormack, Joshua Meador. Story, Homer Brightman, Dick Huemer, Dick Kinney, John Walbridge, Tom Oreb, Dick Shaw, Eric Gurney, Sylvia Holland, T. Hee, Dick Kelsey, Jesse Marsh, Roy Williams, Ed Penner, James Bodrero, Cap Palmer, Erwin Graham. Art supervisor, Mary Blair, Elmer Plummer, John Hench. Animators, Les Clark, Ward Kimball, Milt Kahl, John Sibley, Hal King, Eric Larson, John Lousbery, Oliver M. Johnson, Jr., Fred Moore, Hugh Fraser, Judge Whitaker, Harvey Toombs, Tom Massey, Phil Duncan, Hal Ambro, Jack Campbell, Cliff Nordberg, Bill Justice, Al Bertino, John McManus, Ken O'Brien. Backgrounds, Claude Coats, Art Riley, Ralph Hulett, Merle Cox, Ray Huffine, Albert Dempster, Thelma Witner, Jim Trout. Layout, A. Kendall O'Connor, Hugh Hennesy, Al Zinnen, Ed Benedict, Charles Philippi, Donald Da Gradi, Lance Nolley, Charles Payzant, John Niendorf. Effects animation, George Rowley, Jack Boyd, Andy Engman, Brad Case, Don Patterson. Musical director, Charles Wolcott. Associates Ken Darby, Oliver Wallace, Edward H. Plumb. Process effects, Ub Iwerks. Color consultant: Mique Nelson. Sound: C.O. Slyfield, Robert O. Cook.

Songs "Johnny Fedora and Alice Blue Bonnet," by Allie Wrubel and Ray Gilbert. "All the Cats Join In," by Alec Wilder, Ray Gilbert, and Eddie Sauter. "Without You" by Osvaldo Farres, English lyrics by Ray Gilbert. "Two Silhouettes," by Charles Wolcott and Ray Gilbert. "Casey, the Pride of Them All," by Ray Gilbert, Ken Darby, and Eliot Daniel. "The Martins and the Coys" by Al Cameron and Ted Weems. "Blue Bayou," by Bobby Worth and Ray Gilbert. "After You've Gone," by Henry Creamer and Turner Leighton.   75 minutes.

Presenting the talents of NELSON EDDY, Benny Goodman, Dinah Shore, The Andrews Sisters, Jerry Colonna, Andy Russell, The King's Men, Sterling Holloway, The Pied Pipers, Tatiana Riabouchinska, David Lichine and The Ken Darby Chorus.

NELSON EDDY—The Narrator for
Opera Pathetique, "The Whale Who Wanted To Sing At The Met."
Original Music by Ken Darby. Musical Director, Charles Wolcott.
Nelson as, Willie, The Whale, Signor Tetti-Tatti, Sailors, Sea Gulls, A Trio, The Heavenly Chorus, Assorted Professors, Newsboy, all characters.
Nelson sings: "Short'nin' Bread," "Largo Al Factotum" (Figaro) from *Barber of Seville* by Rossini; Sextette from *Lucia di Lammermoor* by Donizetti; Clown Song from "Punchinello" (take-off on *Pagliacci*); "Tristan Und Isolde" love duet by Wagner; "Devil's Song" from *Mephistopheles* by Boito and the Finale to Act III of *Martha* by Von Flotow.

SYNOPSIS
Songs tell the story for the ten animated segments for this musical cartoon, featuring the swing virtuosity of Benny Goodman and the symphonic bravura of Sergei Prokofiev in episodes like, "Casey at the Bat" and "Blue Bayou" or again "Johnny Fedora and Alice Blue Bonnet" and "All the Cats Join In." Sterling Holloway narrates "Peter and the Wolf" while Jerry Colonna is "Casey at the Bat." "The Martins and the Coys" is a hillbilly ballad about an Ozark mountain feud.

COMMENTS
The twelve minute sequence "The Whale Who Wanted to Sing at the Met" has Nelson narrating this delightful story and singing every role from bass to soprano, climaxing with singing with himself in a chorus larger than ever. It was cleverly done with the considerable talents of both Nelson and the Disney crew. The critics hailed the episode as outstanding.

The New York Times—Bosley Crowther
The picture itself is as disordered as the work of any artist can be. It is an unblushing patchwork assortment of ten different animated "shorts," put together with no rhyme or reason, but like acts in a musical revue. Some are delightful Disney fancies and some are elaborate junk. Watching it is an experience in precipitate ups and downs.

New Yorker
Ninety-odd people, probably more than were required to illuminate the Book of Kells, are credited with having put together *Make Mine Music* under the supervision of Walt Disney. They have labored, but they have not brought forth another Mickey Mouse. Instead, they have fashioned an uneven musical melange, which starts out with an elementary and not too comical cartoon based on the feuding of the Martins and the Coys, and wanders through pompous tone poems, saccharine ballads, and bobby-sox nonsense to a smash tomato finish, in which Nelson Eddy, singing in all kinds of voices, tells the story of 'The Whale Who Wanted to Sing at the Met'...*Make Mine Music* just isn't up to Disney's standards, and nobody is sorrier than I.

202

As Willie, the Whale who wanted to sing at the Met

Northwest Outpost

A Republic Picture   1947

Produced by Herbert J. Yates. Associate producer and director, Allan Dwan. Screenplay by Elizabeth Meehan and Richard Sale. Original story, Angela Stuart. Adaptation by Laird Doyle. Photography by Reggie Lanning. Second unit director, Yakima Canutt. Musical director, Robert Armbruster. Orchestrations by Ned Freeman. First assistant director, Johnny Grubbs. Recording directors, Earl Crain, Sr. and Howard Wilson. Art Directors, Hilyard Brown and Fred Ritter. Set directors, John McCarthy, Jr. and James Redd. Special effects, Howard and Theodore Lydecker. Costumes by Adele Palmer. Hair styles by Peggy Gray. Makeup supervision, Bob Mark. Technical advisor, Alexis Davidoff. Film editor, Harry Keller.   91 minutes.

Songs "One More Mile to Go," "Raindrops on a Drum," "Love Is the Time," "Nearer and Dearer," "Tell Me With Your Eyes," "Russian Easter Hymn," and "Weary," (convict song). Music by Rudolf Friml. Lyrics by Edward Heyman.

CAST
Captain James Laurence, NELSON EDDY; *Natalie Alanova,* ILONA MASSEY; *Count Igor Savin,* Joseph Schildkraut; *Prince Nickolai,* Hugo Haas; *Princess Tanya,* Elsa Lanchester; *Baroness Kruposny,* Lenore Ulric; *Volkoff,* Peter Whitney; *Olga,* Tamara Shayne; *Kyril,* Erno Verebes; *Baron Kruposny,* George Sorel; *Dovkin,* Rick Vallin; *Chinese Junk Captain,* Henry Brandon; and the American G.I. Chorus.

SYNOPSIS
Natalie arrives at Fort Ross, a 19th Century Russian trading post in California, and is greeted by it's ruler, Nikolai. Although her reasons for coming are remote and clouded

With Ilona Massey

Ilona Massey and Joseph Schildkraut

With Elsa Lanchester and Ilona Massey

in mystery, she is welcomed by Prince Nikolai's wife, Princess Tanya, who introduces her to an American friend, James Laurence, who finds her most attractive. Natalie also meets Count Igor Savin, the exile she had come to find. She had married him in Russia to save her father from a political scandal. Savin forces Natalie to ask the smitten Laurence to help him escape from the Fort. Natalie, who has fallen in love with Laurence, decides at the last minute not to involve him and offers to give Savin her jewels so that he might buy his way out.

Savin bargains with Volkoff, head guard of the convict exiles and Volkoff agrees to help him to freedom and even decides to escape with him. Laurence, having discovered Natalie's interest in Savin, demands that she leave Fort Ross immediately. He leaves to quell an Indian uprising as Savin and Volkoff escape to the harbor and a Chinese Junk which they plan to sail to Russia. In their haste, they lose some of Natalie's jewels. Upon returning Laurence discovers the lost jewels and accuses Natalie of helping Savin escape. She is banished from Fort Ross forever. Natalie boards the junk with the fugitives. But before sailing time, Laurence has traced the escapees to the boat and he and Prince Nikolai kill Savin and Volkoff in a gun battle. Natalie and Laurence are happily reunited.

COMMENTS

This was the last film Nelson did in 1947. It re-united him with the beautiful Ilona Massey who appeared opposite him in *Rosalie* and *Balaliaka*. After this film Nelson established himself as a popular night club performer in an act he did with Gale Sherwood for fifteen years, singing most of the songs he and Jeanette made famous in their films.

Daily Variety

Northwest Outpost is colorful, romantic melodrama backgrounding Rudolf Friml music. The story, though somewhat corny, is more robust in plot than is usually accorded a musical and is good, exciting film fare on its own. Nelson Eddy takes full advantage of the opportunities offered a robust baritone, Ilona Massey accounts excellently for the soprano numbers and the pair prove good box-office lure.

Los Angeles Times

Republic Studios can point with pardonable pride to the restoration of Nelson Eddy to the screen in *Northwest Outpost*. It is in no way one of the greatest film musicals, but it is a good one, different in scope and setting.

With Jose Iturbi

Three Daring Daughters

Technicolor
A Metro-Goldwyn-Mayer Picture   1948

Produced by Joe Pasternak. Directed by Fred M. Wilcox. Screenplay by Albert Mannheimer, Frederick Kohner, Sonja Levien and John Meehan. Photographed by Ray June. Technicolor director, Natalie Kalmus. Associate, Henri Jaffa. Musical direction by Georgie Stoll. Recording director, Douglas Shearer; Art directors, Cedric Gibbons and Preston Ames. Set decorations by Edwin B. Willis. Associate, Arthur Krams. Costume supervision, Irene; associate, Shirley Barker. Makeup created by Jack Dawn. Film editor, Adrienne Fazan.   116 minutes.

Songs   "The Dickey Bird Song," music by Sammy Fain, lyrics by Howard Dietz. "Route 66," music and lyrics by

Bob Troup. "You Made Me Love You," music by James V. Monaco, lyrics by Joe McCarthy.

CAST

Louise Rayton Morgan, JEANETTE MacDONALD; *Himself,* JOSE ITURBI; *Tess Morgan,* JANE POWELL; *Robert Nelson,* Edward Arnold; *Dr. Cannon,* Harry Davenport; *Mrs. Smith,* Moyna MacGill; *Alix Morgan,* Elinor Donahue; *Ilka Morgan,* Ann E. Todd; *Michael Pemberton,* Tom Helmore; *Jonsy,* Kathryn Card; *Specialties,* by Amparo Iturbi and Larry Adler.

With Ann E. Todd, Jane
Powell and Elinor Donahue

With Edward Arnold

208

SYNOPSIS

Louise Morgan, successful career woman, is also the mother of three precocious but charming daughters, for whose benefit she has painted such a glamourous portrait of her divorced husband, their father, that the girls believe their mother may still be in love with him. Louise takes a Caribbean vacation at their insistence, and the sisters make a newspaper tycoon recall their father from his foreign correspondent's job. Meanwhile, Louise, on shipboard, has fallen in love with Jose Iturbi. They marry and return happily to New York, where Louise finds her ex-husband ensconced and determined to re-wed her in order to make his daughters content. Louise's newfound happiness with Iturbi is at stake, and it takes her every feminine and motherly wile to convince her daughters to stay out of her life and convince her ex-husband to go back to being a foreign correspondent.

COMMENTS

Jeanette's first film in four years was back at MGM (where she always truly belonged) and her fifth in Technicolor. Joe Pasternak had been wanting Jeanette back in the MGM fold for sometime. He always had the dream of someday starring Jeanette and his favorite Deanna Durbin, in a film together. He called Jeanette, told her the story of *Three Daring Daughters* over the phone, and got her to accept the role. Filmed in glorious color, given a great amount of care of detail and an outstanding score, the film was not received with the enthusiasm MGM hoped it would be. However, it did make money for the studio and become the twenty-eighth top grossing film of the year.

New York Daily News—Wanda Hale

If there is a movie actress more beautiful than Jeanette MacDonald is in Technicolor on the Capitol's screen in *Three Daring Daughters,* I have yet to see her. After more than four years' absence from the screen as a star, MGM's pet singing artist makes a triumphant return...Jeanette's voice is in just as good, or in better, form than it was when she sang in musical after musical with Nelson Eddy. She plays her role with charming dignity.

Daily Variety

MGM has a top product in *Three Daring Daughters,* a delightful piece of film-making which spells box-office first to last. Picture not only marks the return of Jeanette MacDonald, but provides as slick musical entertainment and a story as charming and heart-warming as the screen has seen in many a day...Miss MacDonald delivers a sensitive performance, and will win new fans for this portrayal.

With Claude Jarman, Jr.

With Lewis Stone, Nicholas Joy and Dwayne Hickman

With Claude Jarman, Jr., and Lassie

The Sun Comes Up

Technicolor
A Metro-Goldwyn-Mayer Picture   1949

Produced by Robert Sisk. Directed by Richard Thorpe. Assistant director, Al Jennings. Screenplay by William Ludwig and Maragaret Fitts; based on the novel *Mountain Prelude* by Marjorie Kinnan Rawlings. Photography by Ray June. Technicolor consultant, Natalie Kalmus; associate, James Gooch. Music score by Andre Previn. Recording director, Douglas Shearer. Art direction by Cedric Gibbons and Randall Duell. Set directions by Edwin B. Willis and Hugh Hunt. Gowns for Miss MacDonald by Irene. Film editor, Irving Warburton.   93 minutes.

Songs "One Fine Day" from the opera, *Madame Butterfly* by Puccini. "Songs My Mother Taught Me," by Dvorak. "Tes Jolies Yeux," by Rabey. "Cousin Ebenezer," music by Andre Previn, lyrics by William Katz. "If You Were Mine," based on "Romance" by Rubenstein.

CAST
Helen Lorfield Winter, JEANETTE MacDONALD; *Thomas I. Chandler,* LLOYD NOLAN; *Jerry,* CLAUDE JARMAN, JR.; *Mr. Willie B. Williegoode,* Percy Kilbride; *Arthur Norton,* Lewis Stone; *Victor Alvord,* Nicholas Joy; *Mrs. Golightly,* Margaret Hamilton; *Mrs. Pope,* Hope Landin; *Susan, the maid,* Esther Somers; *Hank Winter,* Dwayne Hickman; *Junebug,* Teddy Infuhr; *Nurse,* Barbara Billingsley; *Dr. Gage,* Charles Trowbridge; *Doorman,* John A. Butler; *Sally,* Ida Moore; *Dr. Sample,* Paul E. Burns; *Young Man,* Guy Wilkerson; *Cleaver,* Mickey McGuire; and, "Lassie"

With Nicholas Joy conducting the orchestra

With Percy Kilbride

SYNOPSIS

Helen Lorfield Winter, is a famous widowed concert singer who loses her only son in a tragic auto accident, when the boy runs recklessly onto the street after a dog and is hit and killed by a passing car. Unable to tolerate children or pet animals, Helen goes to the Georgia woods to forget and retire from life. Gradually, she is beguiled by Jerry, an orphan boy sent to her cottage by the local orphanage to help her in the more strenuous domestic duties. She fights her growing affection for the boy, but is won over when he is taken ill. The orphanage catches fire, and he is saved from the conflagration by Lassie. She thereupon adopts both the boy and the dog.

COMMENTS

It is usually said that children and animals steal the film away from a star, but not in this case. In *The Sun Comes Up* neither Claude Jarman, Jr. nor Lassie steals the film away from Jeanette. Jeanette sings beautifully and offers a believeable performance in what became her farewell film role.

The Hollywood Reporter

It is perfect family entertainment, and to insure marquee appeal, Metro has armed it with Technicolor, Lassie and Jeanette MacDonald. The three make a most engaging combination...Jeanette MacDonald gives her usual animated and persuasive performance. She is attractively photographed and her voice is heard in "One Fine Day" and a number of charming songs.

Variety

The Sun Comes Up is one of those frankly sentimental tear-jerkers that usually fare rather well in family situations outside the more cosmopolitan areas. It has beautiful color to dress up it's mountain locale and Jeanette MacDonald's smart wardrobe and a number of songs completely in keeping with it's general mood.

The Love Goddesses

A Walter Reade-Sterling Presentation—Released through Continental Distributing.   1964

Produced and written by Saul J. Turell and Graeme Ferguson. Music by Percy Faith. Narrated by Carl King.   87 minutes.

CAST
JEANETTE MacDONALD, Sophia Loren, Marlene Dietrich, Lillian Gish, Louise Glaum, Theda Bara, Mae Marsh, Fannie Ward, Agnes Ayres, Clara Bow, Nita Naldi, Pola Negri, Lya De Putti, Gloria Swanson, Louise Brooks, Hedy Lamarr, Brigette Helm, Greta Garbo, Jean Harlow, Bette Davis, Ruby Keeler, Carole Lombard, Ginger Rogers, Myrna Loy, Mae West, Barbara Stanwyck, Shirley Temple, Lana Turner, Betty Grable, Dorothy Lamour, Rita Hayworth, Elizabeth Taylor, Marilyn Monroe, Hayley Mills, Audrey Hepburn, Heather Sears, Simone Signoret, Brigitte Bardot, Sylvia Syms, Esther Ralston, Claudette Colbert.

SYNOPSIS
This film is projected as the story of sex in the movies through years. It attempts to show the shifting morals and manners of various times as they have been reflected on the screen. Beginning with the good girls and the vamps, it includes the lively heroines and bad girls of the post World War I period, the wide open early thirties, the more restrained depression period, and the frantic fifties and sixties. In this documentary about the changing patterns and vogues of sex and sex goddesses as shown in film history from it's very beginnings to contemporary times, nearly every important female star is favored with a clip showing her at her sexiest best. (Only Mary Pickford, Ann Sheridan and Joan Crawford are noticeably absent, and Garbo is shown only in her pre MGM days). Jeanette MacDonald is featured in a sequence with a song from "Love Me Tonight."

That's Entertainment!

A Metro-Goldwyn Mayer Picture
A United Artists Release   1974

CREDITS
Written, produced and directed by Jack Haley, Jr. Photography by Ernest Laszlo, Russell Metty, Gene Polito, Ennio Guarnieri and Allan Green. Edited by Bud Friedgen and David E. Blewitt. Sound by Hal Watkins, Aaron Rochin, Lyle Burbridge, Harry W. Tetrick and William L. McCaughey. Running time, 132 minutes.

NARRATORS
Liza Minnelli, Elizabeth Taylor, Fred Astaire, James Stewart, Mickey Rooney, Peter Lawford, Frank Sinatra, Debbie Reynolds, Bing Crosby, Gene Kelly and Donald O'Connor.

Jeanette MacDonald and Nelson Eddy were shown briefly in a film clip from *Rose Marie* singing their famous "Indian Love Call."

That's Entertainment, 2

A United Artists Picture   1976

CREDITS
Directed by Gene Kelly. Produced by Saul Chaplin and Daniel Melnick. Written by Leonard Gershe. Music arranged and conducted by Nelson Riddle. Photography by George Folsey. Edited by Bud Friedgen and David E. Blewitt. Sound by Bill Edmondson. Running time, 126 minutes.

NARRATORS
Fred Astaire and Gene Kelly

Jeanette MacDonald and Nelson Eddy were seen performing the "Lover Come Back to Me" number from *New Moon.*

Radio and TV Appearances of Nelson Eddy and Jeanette MacDonald

JEANETTE MacDONALD

Sept. 28, 1929	"Paramount Publix Musical Hour"—songs from Paramount
Nov. 9, 1929	Pictures with various guest stars.
Mar. 8, 1930	
Nov. 15, 1931	"Mobilization for Human Needs."
Oct. 10, 1934	"Atwater Kent Radio Hour."
May 12, 1936	"Party at Pickfair."
June 29, 1936	*Irene,* "Lux Radio Theatre," with Melvyn Douglas, Luis Alberni and Marcella Knapp.
Sept. 26, 1937	"Vicks Open House."
March 20, 1938	"Vicks Open House."
Sept. 16, 1938	"Adoption of the Constitution Program."
Feb. 19, 1939	*A Song for Clotilda,* "Screen Guild Theatre," with Robert Taylor.
1940	"Community Mobilization For Human Needs."
Feb. 21, 1941	*The Wreck on Deliverance,* "Campbell Playhouse."
March 2, 1941	"The Pause That Refreshes on the Air."
Jan. 5, 1942	*Smilin' Through,* "Lux Radio Theatre," with Gene Raymond and Brian Aherne.
Nov. 12, 1942	"Stage Door Canteen" with various guest stars.
April 22, 1943	"Stage Door Canteen" with various guest stars.
Feb. 7, 1944	"Ed Sullivan Entertains."

With Robert Taylor and Paul Muni on NBC's "America Calling" radio broadcast, 1941

Jeanette with Gary Cooper and Eddie Cantor on the radio program "Hollywood Constitution Day."

April 30, 1944	"We the People"—Jeanette spoke from Asheville, North Carolina, describing the city's fine role in war work.
Sept. 9, 1944	"Kenny Baker Radio Show."
Jan. 14, 1945	"Ford Symphony Hour."
April 15, 1945	"F.D.R. Tribute."
May 8, 1945	"V-E Day Program."
Dec. 23, 1945	"Armed Forces Broadcast."
Oct. 13, 1946	"Prudential Family Hour."
Aug. 16, 1948	"Hour of Music."
Aug. 17, 1948	"Hollywood Bowl Concert."
Jan. 17, 1949	*Naughty Marietta,* "Railroad Hour," as guest on Gordon MacRae's show.
Jan. 31, 1949	*Bitter Sweet,* "Railroad Hour," as guest on Gordon MacRae's show.
Mar. 7, 1949	*Merry Widow,* "Railroad Hour," as guest on Gordon MacRae's show.
Apr. 17, 1949	Louella Parson interviews Jeanette MacDonald.
Apr. 18, 1949	*Apple Blossom,* "Railroad Hour," as guest on Gordon MacRae's show.
Nov. 13, 1950	"Voice of Firestone."
Nov. 12, 1952	"This Is Your Life."

Jeanette with Cheryl Walker and Gene Raymond on the radio program "Stage Door Canteen."

March 13, 1955	"Easter Seal Drive."
Feb. 1, 1956	*Prima Donna,* "Screen Directors Playhouse," with a story by Gene Raymond.
March 8, 1956	"The Louella Parsons Story."
April 21, 1957	"Easter Sunrise Service from Hollywood Bowl."
Oct. 31, 1958	"Person to Person" with Gene Raymond and Edward R. Murrow as Host.
Spring 1961	"Tony Thomas Twin Gables Interview."
June 22, 1963	"Flashback" Canadian TV Show.
Dec. 2, 1963	"Hollywood and the Stars."
Jan. 14, 1965	"Movie-Go-Round with Ben Lyon" (BBC) interviewed.

NELSON EDDY

Feb. 17, 1931	"Congress Cigar Show."
Aug. 20, 1931	"Stadium Concerts."
Oct. 25, 1931	"Congress Cigar Show."
Jan. 27, 1933	"Socony-Vacuum Show."
June 9, 1933	"Socony-Vacuum Show."

March 29, 1934	"Ford Sunday Evening Hour."
March 31, 1935	"Ford Sunday Evening Hour."
May 11, 1935	"California Melodies."
Sept. 27, 1936	"Vick's Open House."
March 21, 1937	"Vick's Open House."
April 18, 1937	"Ford Sunday Evening Hour."
April 3, 1938	"Ford Sunday Evening Hour."
May 28, 1939	"Screen Guild Theatre."
Dec. 24, 1939	*The Bluebird,* "Screen Guild Theatre."
Dec. 22, 1940	*"The Juggler of Our Lady,* "Screen.Guild Theatre."
Dec. 21, 1941	*"The Juggler of Our Lady,* "Screen Guild Theatre."
April 29, 1942	"The Old Gold Show."
June 3, 1942	"The Old Gold Show."
Dec. 21, 1942	*"The Juggler of Our Lady,* "Screen Guild Theatre."
Jan. 20, 1943	"The New Old Gold Show."
Sept. 13, 1943	*Phantom of the Opera,* "Lux Radio Theatre," with Susanna Foster and Basil Rathbone.
Sept. 20, 1944	"The Electric Hour."
Oct. 29, 1944	"New York Philharmonic Symphony."
Oct. 30, 1944	"Open House."
Dec. 13, 1944	"The Electric Hour."
Dec. 17, 1944	"The Electric Hour."
May 8, 1945	"V-E Day Program."
July 1, 1945	"The Electric Hour."
Sept. 9, 1945	"The Electric Hour."
Sept. 23, 1945	"Stars in the Afternoon."

Dec. 9, 1945	"Jerome Kern Memorial."
Dec. 23, 1945	"New York Philharmonic Symphony."
June 9, 1946	"The Electric Hour."
Aug. 26, 1946	"General Electric Houseparty."
June 14, 1951	"The Alan Young Show."
October 4, 1951	"The Alan Young Show."
May 22, 1960	"Ed Sullivan Show," with Gale Sherwood.
Dec. 1, 1961	"Dinah Shore Show."
Apr. 25, 1963	"Today Show" with Gale Sherwood.
Mar. 27, 1965	"Hollywood Palace" with Gale Sherwood.
July 15, 1965	"Dialing for Dollars," Minneapolis, with Gale Sherwood.
Dec. 31, 1966	"Guy Lombardo New Year's Eve Show" from New York.

JEANETTE AND NELSON

June 12, 1944	*Naughty Marietta*, "Lux Radio Theatre."
Sept. 4, 1944	*Maytime*, "Lux Radio Theatre."
April 22, 1945	"Electric Hour"—Jeanette as a guest on Nelson Eddy's show.
Dec. 16, 1945	"Electric Hour"—Jeanette as guest on Nelson Eddy's Show
March 25, 1946	*Sweethearts*, "Lady Esther Screen Guild Theatre."
Dec. 23, 1946	"Electric Hour,"—Jeanette as a guest on Nelson Eddy's show.
June 23, 1947	*Rose Marie*, "Screen Guild Theatre."
Dec. 15, 1947	*Sweethearts*, "Screen Guild Theatre."
Sept. 16, 1948	"Kraft Music Hall"—Jeanette as a guest on Nelson Eddy's show.
Dec. 21, 1955	"The Big Parade" Show.
Feb. 11, 1956	"The Big Parade" Show.
Sept. 25, 1957	"The Big Record" Show.

Movie Duets
Sung by Jeanette MacDonald and Nelson Eddy

Naughty Marietta
"Ah, Sweet Mystery of Life"
Finale, "Ah Sweet Mystery of Life"

Rose Marie
"Indian Love Call"
Finale, "Indian Love Call"

Maytime
"Carry Me Back to Old Virginia"
"Santa Lucia"
"Will You Remember"
"Czaritza"
Finale, "Will You Remember"

Girl of the Golden West
"Mariachie"
Finale, "Senorita"

Sweethearts
"Every Lover Must Meet His Fate"
"Sweethearts"
Finale, "Every Lover Must Meet His Fate"
Encore, "Sweethearts"
"Pretty as a Picture"
"Game of Love"
"Breath of Springtime" ("My Heart's True Blue")
Reprise, "Every Lover Must Meet His Fate"
Reprise, "Sweethearts"
"Little Gray Home in the West"
Finale, "Sweethearts"

New Moon
"Wanting You"
"Our Sincere Congratulations" ("Marianne")
"Lover Come Back to Me"
Finale, "Wanting You"

Bittersweet
"I'll See You Again"
"What Is Love"
"What Is Love"—not complete
"In a Sweet Little Cafe" ("Dear Little Cafe")
"Call of Life"—background only
"What Is Love"
Finale, "I'll See You Again

I Married An Angel
"I'll Tell the Man on the Street"
"Spring Is Here"
Opera Montage
Finale, "I Married An Angel,"
"I'll Tell The Man on the Street,"
and "Spring Is Here"

Jeanette MacDonald Discography

(All albums are 33 1/3 rpm long playing records unless otherwise noted.

RCA LCT-16   **OPERETTA FAVORITES**—Indian Love Call, Farewell to Dreams, Will You Remember?, Ah, Sweet Mystery of Life, I'm Falling in Love With Someone.

RCA LPM-1738
LSP-1738   **FAVORITES IN HI-FI**—Will You Remember?, Ah, Sweet Mystery of Life, Wanting You, Indian Love Call, Giannina Mia, Italian Street Song, Beyond the Blue Horizon, The Breeze and I, Rosalie, While My Lady Sleeps, Stouthearted Men, Rose Marie.

RCA LPV-526   **JEANETTE MacDONALD & NELSON EDDY**—Italian Street Song, Ah, Sweet Mystery of Life, Indian Love Call, Will You Remember?, I'll See You Again, Tramp, Tramp, Tramp, 'Neath the Southern Moon, I'm Falling in Love With Someone, The Mounties, Rose Marie, Who Are We to Say?, Sweetheart Waltz, Summer Serenade, Lover Come Back to Me, Song of Love.

EVEREST EPA-5053   **JEANETTE MacDONALD & NELSON EDDY**—Indian Love Call, Ah, Sweet Mystery of Life, Will You Remember?, Wanting You. (45 RPM)

EVEREST EPA 5113   **MOVIE MEMORIES**—Lover, Come Back to Me, San Francisco, Rose Marie, The Mounties. (45 RPM)

EVEREST ERA-220   Rose Marie, Indian Love Call, Ah, Sweet Mystery of Life, The Mounties. (45 RPM)

PELICAN LP 103   **NEW MOON** and **I MARRIED AN ANGEL** (Motion Picture Soundtrack).

PELICAN LP 116   **MAYTIME**—Radio Broadcast.

PELICAN LP 117   **NAUGHTY MARIETTA**—Radio Broadcast.

RCA M-642   **JEANETTE MacDONALD IN SONG** (78 rpm)
2047   Do Not Go My Love, When I Have Sung My Songs.
2049   Ave Maria, Les Filles de Cadiz.
2050   Il Etait un Roi de Thule, Air des Bijoux.
2055   Annie Laurie, Comin Through The Rye, Let Me Always Sing, From The Land of the Sky Blue Water.

RCA M-847   **SMILIN' THROUGH** (78 rpm)
18315   Smilin' Through, A Little Love, a Little Kiss.
18316   Kerry Dance, Ouvre Ton Coeur.
18317   Land of Hope and Glory, Drink to Me Only With Thine Eyes.

RCA LM-2908   **JEANETTE MacDONALD OPERA AND OPERETTA FAVORITES**—Waltz Song, Il Etait un Roi de Thule, Depuis le Jour, Un Bel Di Vedremo, Mi Chiamano Mimi, Ouvre Ton Coeur, Les Filles de Cadiz, Romany Life, They Didn't Believe Me, Smoke Gets in Your Eyes, Donkey Serenade, Giannina Mia.

CAMDEN CAL-325   **SMILIN' THROUGH**—Drink To Me Only With Thine Eyes, Ave Maria, Ciribiribin, Italian Street Song, One Kiss, Zigeuner, Vilia, I'll See You Again, Lover, Come Back to Me, Parlez Moi d'Amour, Smilin' Through, Songs My Mother Taught Me.

RCA CAMDEN-750 JEANETTE MacDONALD SINGS SONGS OF FAITH AND INSPIRATION—Holy City, Agnus Dei, Songs My Mother Taught Me, Abide With Me, Battle Hymn of the Republic, Ave Maria, O Lord Most Holy, Nearer, My God, to Thee, Land of Hope and Glory, The Old Refrain.

RCA LM-62 ROMANTIC MOMENTS—When You're Away, Parlez Moi d'Amour, One Alone, Ah, Sweet Mystery of Life, Will You Remember, San Francisco.

RCA Y-327 CINDERELLA—a children's musical recording.

RCA M-1217 ROMANTIC MELODIES (78 rpm)
10-1414 I'll See You Again, Zigeuner.
10-1415 Summertime, The Man I Love.
10-1416 I Love You Truly, A Perfect Day.
10-1417 Romance (Debussy), Beau Soir.

RCA M-1071 OPERETTA FAVORITES (78 rpm)
10-1242 Romany Life, Sweethearts Waltz.
10-1243 They Didn't Believe Me, Smoke Gets in Your Eyes.
10-1244 Donkey Serenade, Giannina Mia.

RCA M-996 RELIGIOUS SONGS (78 rpm)
10-1168 Nearer, My God to Thee, Abide With Me.
10-1169 Holy City, Agnus Dei.
10-1170 Oh, Lord, Most Holy, Battle Hymn of the Republic.

RCA M-991 UP IN CENTRAL PARK (with Robert Merrill) (78 rpm)
10-1153 Carousel in the Park, It Doesn't Cost You Anything to Dream.

10-1154 Fireman's Bride, Close as Pages in a Book.
10-1155 The Big Back Yard, When You Walk in the Room.

RCA Vic-1515 JEANETTE MacDONALD SINGS "SAN FRANCISCO" AND OTHER SILVER SCREEN FAVORITES—San Francisco, One Alone, Will You Remember?, Ah, Sweet Mystery of Life, When You're Away, Indian Love Call, Ciribiribin, Only a Rose, Beyond the Blue Horizon, One Night of Love, Merry Widow Waltz, Italian Street Song.

Nelson Eddy Discography

COL-AA1-37   **THE DESERT SONG** (with Doretta Morrow—French Military Marching Song, Romance, Then You Will Know, I Want a Kiss, The Desert Song, Let Love Go, One Flower, One Alone, Sabre Song, The Riff Song, Margot.

CAMDEN CAL-492   **NELSON EDDY FAVORITES**—Ah, Sweet Mystery of Life, The Rosary, Love's Old Sweet Song, Oh Promise Me, a Dream, When I Grow Too Old to Dream, Trees, Auf Wiedersehen, The Hills of Home, A Perfect Day, Tramp, Tramp, Tramp.

COL HL 7151   **BECAUSE**—Because, Trees, Sylvia, A Perfect Day, Berceuse, Smilin' Through, At Dawning, The Sweetest Story Ever Told, I Love You Truly, Serenade.

COL HL 7254   **THE LORD'S PRAYER**—The Rosary, Holy Art Thou, The Palms, Panis Angelicus, The Holy City, Agnus Dei, Ave Maria, The Lord's Prayer.

EVEREST LPBR 9002   **NELSON EDDY AND GALE SHERWOOD** (all duets)—Wunderbar, You and the Night and the Music, The Song Is You, This Is My Beloved, Our Love, One Alone, One Night of Love, I Love You, If I Loved You, Shall We Dance, You Are Love.

COL ML 4099   **SONGS OF STEPHEN FOSTER**—Come Where My Love Lies Dreaming, Old Folks at Home, The Merry Merry Month of May, Angelina Baker, Old Black Joe, Oh, Boys, Carry Me 'Long, My Brudder Gum, De Camptown Races, My Old Kentucky Home, Old Dog Tray, Dolly Day, Louisiana Belle, Jeannie With the Light Brown Hair, Massa's in De Cold, Cold Ground, There's No Such Girl as Mine, Nelly Bly, Open Thy Lattice, Love, Beautiful Dreamer, Fairy Belle, Don't Bet Your Money on de Shanghai, Oh, Susanna, Come Where My Love Lies Dreaming.

COL GB 3   **ROMANTIC MOMENTS** from *Rose Marie, New Moon, Naughty Marietta* (with Dorothy Kirsten, Nadine Connor and Eleanor Steber)—Rose Marie and Indian Love Call with Dorothy Kirsten; Wanting You with Eleanor Steber; Totem Tom Tom with Dorothy Kirsten; Softly, as in a Morning Sunrise, Door of My Dreams, Lover, Come Back to Me, with Eleanor Steber; I'm Falling in Love With Someone, Ah, Sweet Mystery of Life with Nadine Connor; Italian Street Song solo by Nadine Connor; 'Neath the Southern Moon, One Kiss with Eleanor Steber.

COL HL 7142   **STOUT HEARTED MEN**—Tramp, Tramp, Tramp, Stout Hearted Men, Riders in the Sky, Water Boy, Without a Song, Song of the Flea, The Cork Leg, Rodger Young, The Laughing Song, The Mounties.

EVEREST LPBR 9004 SDBR 8004   **A STARRY NIGHT**—Tonight We Love, It's Love, Love, Love; The Lamp Is Low, Story of a Starry Night, My Reverie, Love Serenade, 'Till the End of Time, Stranger in Paradise, Strange Music, As Years Years Go By, Full Moon and Empty Arms, If You Are But a Dream.

COL M-690   **NORTHWEST OUTPOST** (78 rpm)

7563M Raindrops on a Drum, One More Mile To Go.

7564M Nearer And Dearer, Love Is The Time.

7565M Tell Me With Your Eyes, Russian Easter Hymn.

COL MM-724 THE STUDENT PRINCE (with Rise Stevens) (78 rpm)

4508M Golden Days, Come Boys, sung by Rise Stevens.

4509M Drinking Song, Just We Two with Rise Stevens.

4510M Deep in My Heart, Dear, with Rise Stevens; Serenade.

COL MM-1017 SONGS FOR CHRISTMAS (78 rpm)

4690 M Jingle Bells, Joy to the World, Deck the Halls, Silent Night.

4691 M Good King Wenceslas, Hark the Herald Angels Sing, The First Noel.

4692 M Away in the Manger, God Rest Ye Merry, Gentlemen, White Christmas.

4693 M O, Holy Night, O' Come All Ye Faithful, O, Little Town of Bethlehem.

EVEREST EPA 4348 OUT OF THE NIGHT In the Still of the Night, Isn't This a Night For Love, Somewhere In the Night, Out of the Night. (45 rpm)

COL A-482 EXCERPTS from *The Chocolate Soldier* and *The Student Prince,* with Rise Stevens (45 rpm)

7-1521 My Hero, While My Lady Sleeps, Deep in My Heart Dear, Just We Two.

7-1522 The Chocolate Soldier, Forgive, Ti-Ra-La-La, Sympathy.

COL M-440 PATTER SONGS from Gilbert and Sullivan, Vol. I (78 rpm)

4271 M My Object All Sublime, Oh, a Private Buffoon.

4272 M Lord Chancellor's Nightmare Song,

My Name Is John Wellington Wells.

4273 M Major General's Song, I Am the Monarch of the Sea, When I Was a Lad.

COL M-507 CONCERT FAVORITES (78 rpm)

17328D Trade Winds, Mother Carey.

17329D Short'nin Bread, Water-Boy.

17330D Route Marchin', Boots

17331D Se Vuol Ballare, Non Piu Andrai.

COL M-571 BY REQUEST (78 rpm)

4315 M Without a Song, Great Day.

4316 M Red Rosey Bush, Frog Went a-Courtin.

4317 M Because, My Message.

4318 M Strange Music, I Love You

COL MM-640 THE WHALE WHO WANTED TO SING AT THE MET (78 rpm)

4345 M Side 1: Three Blind Mice; Side 6: Finale to Martha, Act 3.

4346 M Side 2: Shortn'in Bread; Side 5: Various excerpts.

4347 M Side 3: Largo Al Factotum; Side 4: Sextet, Lucia di Lammermoor.

COL M-670 PATTER SONGS from Gilbert and Sullivan, Vol. II (78 rpm)

4370 M If You're Anxious for to Shine, When a Felon's Not Engaged, When the Foreman Bares His Steel.

4371 M My Boy, You May Take It From Me, When I, Good Friends.

4372 M Rising Early in the Morning, If You Give Me Your Attention, Whene'er I Spoke.

COL MM-1033 OKLAHOMA with Kaye Ballard, Wilton Clary, Virginia Haskins, Portia Nelson, David Atkinson, David Morris and Lee Cass (78 rpm)

4711 M Overture—Oklahoma—Nelson and Chorus.

4712 M Oh, What a Beautiful Morning

(Nelson); Kansas City (Portia Nelson & Wilton Clary; All Er Nothin' (Kay Ballard, Wilton Clary.

4713 M Surrey With the Fringe (Nelson, Virginia Haskins, Portia Nelson), Out of My Dreams (Virginia Haskins);

4714 M I Cain't Say No (Kaye Ballard); Lonely Room (Lee Cass).

4715 M Many a New Day (Virginia Haskins); Poor Jud Is Daid (Nelson with Lee Cass).

4716 M It's a Scandal, It's an Outrage (David Morris); People Will Say We're in Love (Nelson with Virginia Haskins and Portia Nelson).

COL MM 930 **LOVE SONGS FROM FOREIGN LANDS** (78 rpm)

4621 M Der Kuss, Kit Kene Elvenni.

4622 M Por Eso Te Quiero, Dansando O Samba.

4623 M Si Tu Veux, Mignonne; Matus Moya Matus.

4624 M Niet, Niet, Ya Nie Khotcho, Ricordati Di Me.

RCA C-27 **TWELVE BELOVED AMERICAN SONGS** (78 rpm)

V4366 Trees, By the Water of Minnetonka.

V4367 Smilin' Through, A Dream.

V4368 Sylvia, Thy Beaming Eyes.

V4369 A Perfect Day, At Dawning.

V4370 Oh, Promise Me, The Rosary.

V4371 The Hills of Home, Deep River.

COL X-150 **FOUR INDIAN LOVE CALL LYRICS** (78 rpm)

17161D The Temple Bells, Less Than the Dust.

17162D Kashmiri Song, Till I Wake.

COL MM-873 **A SONG JAMBOREE** (78 rpm)

4584M Riders in the Sky, The Laughing Song.

4585M The Wreck of the Julie Plante, Sailormen.

4586M Captain Stratton's Fancy, The Cork Leg.

4587M Shadrack, Tower of Babel.

COL A-1644 **REQUESTS** (45 rpm)

7-1421 Because, Danny Boy, Ich Liebe Dich (Grieg), Strange Music.

COL A-1598 **SONGS OF PRAYER** (45 rpm)

7-1343 The Lord's Prayer, Legend-Christ Had a Garden, The Lost Chord, Children's Evening Prayer.